C000230017

VICTORIA BLAKE

Ruth Ellis

the national archives

First published in 2008 by
The National Archives
Kew, Richmond
Surrey, TW9 4DU, UK
www.nationalarchives.gov.uk

The National Archives
brings together the Public Record Office,
Historical Manuscripts Commission,
Office of Public Sector Information
and Her Majesty's Stationery Office.

A catalogue card for this book is available from the British Library.

ISBN 978 1 905615 19 3

Cover illustrations: portraits of Ruth Ellis (Bettmann/Corbis)
and David Blakely (Popperfoto)
Jacket design and page typesetting by Goldust Design
Page design and plate section typesetting by Ken Wilson | point 918
Picture research by Gwen Campbell
Printed in Germany by
Bercker Graphischer Betrieb GmbH & Co

Contents

———

I blame the whole sequence of events on the fact of such an unhappy experience of three bad men ...

Ruth Ellis's father

My Dear Daughter was not half as bad as she seems. She had a good and loving nature and normally would not hurt anyone ... I am sure when she committed this crime she must have been half demented.

Ruth Ellis's mother

Dance with a Stranger

On 10 April 1955 Ruth Ellis stood outside the Magdala, a pub in Hampstead, waiting for her lover David Blakely to emerge. As he stepped from the pub with his friend Clive Gunnell and began to open the door to his car, she took a .38 Smith & Wesson out of her handbag and fired the first of six shots. Four entered Blakely's body, one ricocheted into the base of the thumb of a passer-by and the last was never found. It was later discovered that one of the bullets had been shot from a distance of three inches into Blakely's back.

Given a crime as shocking as this, it is not surprising that the case went on to grip the national imagination. It spawned innumerable books, including Arthur Koestler's *Reflections on Hanging*, a Cannes Festival award-winning film, *Dance with a Stranger* (1985), starring Miranda Richardson and Rupert Everett, and several television documentaries. It was also said to have influenced the famous Diana Dors film, *Yield to the Night* (1956), which was used in the campaign to abolish capital punishment.

The story of this crime can be approached from a number of different angles. First, it is the personal story of a tempestuous relationship between Ellis, a 28-year-old mother of two and nightclub hostess, and Blakely, a playboy racing driver. This relationship was characterized by sexual obsession, love, hate, violence and jealousy—all culminating in a brutal crime of passion. Secondly, it is a story involving that quintessential British obsession, class—the story of an 'unmitigated cad' from a privileged background and a working-class woman earning a living on the edges of prostitution. Thirdly, it is the legal story of probably one of the shortest murder trials in British legal history. And finally it is the political story of the awakening of the national conscience and the ensuing campaign for the abolition of capital punishment. The wave of revulsion that followed Ruth Ellis's hanging led to the introduction of the defence of diminished responsibility in the Homicide Act in 1957 and the abolition of the death penalty in 1969.

What, then, were the circumstances leading up to this seemingly atrocious crime? And who was the woman who had so cold-bloodedly shot her lover down?

GENTLEMEN PREFER BLONDES

Ruth Ellis was born in Rhyl in Wales on 9 October 1926, the fourth of six children. Her father, Arthur Hornby (his performing name was Neilson), was a musician, a cellist who had fallen on hard times when the emergence of the talkies meant there was no longer any need for live music in the cinema. The town was conveniently close to Liverpool, where he managed for a while to get work on the cruise ships. Ruth's mother, Bertha (see plate 14), was half French and half Belgian. Orphaned at two years old, she had been raised by Catholic nuns and came to England as a refugee during the First World War, wrapped in a blanket and with no shoes on her feet.

The marriage was not a happy one, undermined as it was by Arthur's ineffectual attempts to find employment, his growing violence and his sexual abuse of Ruth and her older sister Muriel. The family moved frequently, ostensibly for Arthur to find work, but presumably also to avoid too many questions being asked about what was happening to his children. They moved to Basingstoke and Reading, Arthur being employed as a porter in a mental hospital and a caretaker. In 1941 he got a job as a chauffeur in London and the whole family went with him.

The war-torn capital was full of GIs, with money in their pockets and looking for a good time. Ruth was 15 years old, pretty and fed up with her repressive home life. She worked as a waitress, then in a munitions factory and in the Oxo factory in Southwark. Her motto during this time was 'a short life and a gay one', according to Lawrence Marks and Tony van den Bergh in *Ruth Ellis: A Case of Diminished Responsibility*. She had dyed her hair blonde, in accordance with the popular sentiment that 'gentlemen prefer blondes'. And even though she was short-sighted she refused to wear her glasses. She was also a gutsy young woman. When the Ellises' house suffered a direct hit in a bombing raid, she dug her father out of the rubble and saved his life.

After she spent an eight-week period in bed with rheumatic fever, a doctor told Ruth that she should take as much exercise as possible, and suggested dancing. She had already started going out to clubs in the West End but now she threw herself into this activity with renewed vigour. She quit the Oxo factory and enrolled in a drama school in Richmond, then sang in a band and worked as an usherette at a cinema. She was ambitious and keen to make something of her life. She wanted to be more than a factory worker.

While working as a photographer's assistant at the Locarno Ballroom in 1943, Ruth met a French-Canadian soldier called Clare Andrea McCallum. She was now 17 years old. He was ten years her senior and willing to splash out money on dresses, jewellery and flowers, especially red carnations. It seems that they were genuinely in love. Then she became pregnant and Clare said he would marry her. Ruth's mother, suspicious of the ensuing delays, wrote to Clare's commanding officer only to find that the soldier was married with three children. Clare was quickly shipped home, sending Ruth a huge bunch of red carnations on the day he left.

She went to a nursing home near Carlisle and gave birth to a son, Andre Clare McCallum (also called Andrea, Andria and

Andy in various sources), on 15 September 1944. Back in London the baby was handed over to Muriel, who already had three children of her own, and Ruth returned to work.

An advertisement soon caught her eye: 'Wanted. Model for Camera Club. Nude but artistic poses. No experience required. Highest references available. Confidential' (Marks and van den Bergh). She applied for an interview, stripped and was engaged on the spot. In her book *Ruth Ellis: My Sister's Secret Life*, Muriel Jakubait disputes any description of the Camera Club as being filled with lecherous men holding cameras that contained no film. Whatever the case, the job was a turning point in Ruth's life, because it brought her into contact with Morris 'Maury' Conley.

A MONSTER WITH THE MAYFAIR TOUCH

On 11 December 1955 Duncan Webb wrote in *The People*: 'Right in the centre of corruption in the West End of London stands the figure of Morris Conley. I hereby name him as Britain's biggest vice boss and the chief source of the tainted money that nourishes the evils of London night life.' He went on to describe Conley as 'a monster with the Mayfair touch'. Conley was just the kind of man to thrive in the turmoil of the post-war years. When Ruth met him he was buying up new blocks of flats, patching up derelict buildings and renting them out for exorbitant sums. He was also running four West End clubs.

Conley registered the flats in the name of his wife and then let them to the girls who worked as hostesses in his clubs. The girls got a flat, a job, tips, expenses and free evening dresses. The rent was steep but could be paid if they were willing to sleep with the clients and other men that he might put their way. Basically Conley was making a living from prostitution, although that was not how it looked, because his wife was receiving the rent money and the girls weren't on the streets. He was, as Marks and van den Bergh state, 'a dealer in flesh'—and the Camera Club was a 'fertile source of merchandise'.

Conley visited the Camera Club, saw how confidently Ruth handled herself with the male photographers and knew that she would do well in his clubs. He invited her out for a drink at Carroll's Club in Duke Street and soon afterwards she began working for him. As a hostess she would sit with a client for £5 provided he could also pay £3 for a bottle of champagne. She didn't have to sleep with him—she was being paid for her company and the champagne—but if he wanted more and she was minded to accommodate him, an arrangement could be reached. As a factory worker Ruth would have been on a salary of £4 a week; now she was earning £20 plus personal presents.

The clubs were filled with wealthy black marketeers, socialites and servicemen waiting to be discharged from the forces. Ruth was leading a wealthier, more glamorous life than any she had ever known: she had found something she was good at and which brought financial rewards. And it was at the Court Club that in 1950 she first met George Ellis.

THIS BRUTE OF A MAN

George Ellis was known in the Club as 'the mad dentist' and as a generous buyer of champagne. He became obsessed with Ruth, but at first she would have nothing to do with him outside the club. One night when she failed to meet him at the Hollywood Club he had his face slashed with a razor; the cut required eight stitches. Feeling responsible, Ruth agreed to go out with him.

On the plus side, Ellis was an educated man with a decent profession. Unfortunately he was also an unstable, violent alcoholic whose first wife had left him because of his cruelty. Ruth persuaded him to go into Warlingham Park Psychiatric Hospital to be treated by a Dr Rees. George dried out and was discharged, and on 8 November 1950 he and Ruth were married. Ruth was 24 years old, George 41. Perhaps she saw in him the chance of respectability and a step up the social ladder, a chance to establish some sort of settled family life for herself and Andre, the sort of life that she had never experienced as a child.

George found a job in a dental practice in Warsash, Southampton, and promptly went straight back to his first love: the bottle. In a statement Ruth's mother gave to Ruth's solicitor, John Bickford, two weeks before her daughter was hanged, she said about George:

He was an alcoholic drinker and turned out to be a cruel man…
It was a lonely house, my daughter sitting by herself night
after night, her husband coming home in a taxi because he was
unable to stand he was so drunk. On one of these occasions he
told my Daughter to go into the kitchen. Once she was there he
locked the door. He pulled her hair and banged her head
against the Wall six or seven times. After that seen [sic] she
started bleeding from the nose. Losing pints of blood. She
suffered from terrible head ages [sic] for a long time. On
another occasion he ill-treaded [sic] her by knocking her on the
floor and kicking her. She was black and blue all over. She ran
into the garden and stayed behind a bush all night. She was
terrified of him and ran away from him the next day. She stayed
home with me for three days. (HO 291/237)

Within a fortnight of Ruth's return to him the same thing had
happened and she was back at her mother's:

Both her eyes were swollen. She had a bald patch on the left
side of her head. Her legs were bruised. She was a very sick
girl. I put her to bed and kept her there for several days. I
refused to let her return to this Brute of a man.

Five months after the wedding George was fired from his job.
Ruth was now pregnant and George returned to Warlingham
Park Hospital. She had been consumed with jealousy while
living in Warsash; when she visited her husband at the hospital
she accused him of having an affair with his female doctor and
became so hysterical she had to be physically restrained. Marks

and van den Bergh allege that she was given sedatives by Dr Rees, claiming that from this point on she took drugs as a treatment for nerves and that she was taking these at the time of the murder.

Ruth returned to London. In May, four months pregnant, she was given a small part in a Diana Dors film, *Lady Godiva Rides Again*, a comedy about beauty contests; she was an extra playing one of the contestants. On 2 October 1951 she gave birth to a baby girl, Georgina.

Of this time in Ruth's life, Mr Leon Simmons, a legal executive with Mishcon's (Ruth's civil solicitor, who dealt with her divorce), wrote to the Home Office on 30 June 1955:

> I have no doubt at all that Mrs Ellis suffered considerably both
> mentally and physically at the hands of her husband …
> following the birth of Georgina Mrs Ellis was in a hopeless
> financial position and I recall that at one stage she was in fact
> walking the street with Georgina in a pram looking for accom-
> modation. (HO 291/237)

Ruth was 25 years old with two children to support. Her marriage to George was over. Without telling her, on discharge from hospital he went to Warrington in Lancashire where he had met his first wife, and took a job as a school's dentist. He left instructions with his solicitor that Georgina should be adopted. Ruth wouldn't agree to this. Georgina was handed over to Muriel and her mother, and Ruth went back to work. Conley welcomed her with open arms: this time he made her manageress of the Little Club in Brompton Road and gave her the use of the flat above it. Her basic salary was £15 per week plus commission on bar sales and an entertainment allowance of £10 a week.

Ruth's marriage to George Ellis was undermined by many of the same elements that would prove so disastrous in her next relationship: unpredictability, jealousy and violence, and a weak, alcoholic partner from a middle-class background who both tantalized and dashed her hopes of social respectability. These factors were to combine with the even more incendiary ones of love, lust and sexual obsession when Ruth met David Blakely.

CHAPTER ONE

———

A Poor Twisted Boy

▬▬

David Blakely was described by one of his associates, Cliff Davis, as 'a good looking, well-educated, supercilious shit', who 'wasn't averse to poncing, and certainly ponced off Ruth' (Marks and van den Bergh). Photos of Blakely show a boyish, rather weak face (see plate 2). His father was a GP in Sheffield and he came from a well-off middle-class family. In 1940, when David was 11, his parents divorced, and his mother quickly remarried Humphrey Cook, a wealthy car racing enthusiast. David got on well with his stepfather, sharing his enthusiasm for racing. He had a mediocre career at school (Shrewsbury) and in the army (Highland Light Infantry), before Humphrey found him a job as a management trainee at the Hyde Park Hotel. His income was supplemented by money from his mother and stepfather, but if they hoped that he would buckle down they were to be disappointed. David had no interest in hotels except as a useful milieu for picking up women. As he said to Cliff Davis, 'Work drives me potty' (Robert Hancock, *Ruth Ellis: The Last Woman to be Hanged*). All he was interested in was car racing, an obsession fuelled when his stepfather gave him a second-hand HRG sports car. In 1952 his father died and left him £7,000, and it wasn't long before he was fired from his hotel job. Arriving at the hotel the following day, he ordered himself a gin and tonic and lounged conspicuously in the bar.

The Steering Wheel Club was where all the top racing drivers went, including Stirling Moss, and it was a magnet for David. He also frequented Maury Conley's clubs, and it was at Carroll's Club in August 1953 that he first met Ruth. Her comment on him was: 'I hope never to see that little shit again' (Hancock). When they next met it was at the Little Club; within a fortnight they were lovers and he had moved into Ruth's flat. According to Marks and van den Bergh, David, ever the gentleman, was quickly boasting to Cliff Davis that she was one of the 'finest fucks' in town.

David Blakely was by all accounts a mediocrity, an inadequate man out of his depth in any conversation that did not involve racing cars. He couldn't hold his drink and was a physical coward, who would squirt a soda siphon over someone and then run and cower behind the bar, begging everyone else to protect him. But the 'little boy lost' routine was successful with some women. At this stage he was engaged to Linda Dawson from Yorkshire; their official engagement was announced in *The Times* on 11 November 1953. He was also seeing a cinema usherette and at another point a tall American model. Ruth was still married to Ellis, so initially the relationship was casual on both sides. By Christmas 1953 Ruth was pregnant by him, but she later summed up her attitude as follows in her proof of evidence (the long statement she gave to her solicitor laying out the case from her point of view, contained in HO 291/237): 'I certainly did not intend to take advantage of such a position. My pregnancy was in fact terminated on or about February 1954.'

Humphrey Cook had bought a big house, Old Park, in Penn, Buckinghamshire. David had a flat there and got a job with Silicon Pistons, a nearby engineering company. He moved back and forth between Ruth's flat and Penn, where he even had his old nanny to look after him. He had all the financial security available to someone of his wealthy middle-class background. Ruth's security lay in her job at the club.

THE FINDLATERS

With the money he had inherited, David decided to design and build the prototype for a fleet of sports cars. He turned to his friend Ant Findlater for help (see plate 13). The two men had first met in 1951 when Ant had been working for Aston Martin. Now David suggested he pay Ant £10 a week to work for him. Ant's wife, Carole, was a journalist who had worked as a sub-editor on *Woman* magazine: Harry Ashbrook, another journalist, described her as 'a powerhouse of ambition and energy while Ant seemed happy fiddling with carburettors' (Hancock).

On 19 June 1955 Carole Findlater was interviewed by
Ashbrook for the *Sunday Pictorial*. A copy of his notes of the
meeting were forwarded by Ruth's solicitor, John Bickford, to
the Home Office on 11 July. Carole describes her relationship
with David as follows:

> Three years ago I left my husband to live with David Blakely.
> We were in love ... or at least felt we were but there were a
> number of difficulties, mainly financial. After a few months I
> returned to my husband. I told him the truth and there was a
> reconciliation. I came to regard David as a dear and close friend
> but not my lover. Yet I knew Ruth was jealous. She never
> mentioned my earlier affair with David to me but I felt she
> disliked me. She didn't like him coming to the flat so often.
>
> (HO 291/238)

The two men were not going to allow an affair to come between
them. Hancock states that when Carole told David that Ant
knew of the affair, he said with typical gallantry: 'You stupid
bitch... who the bloody hell will tune my car now?' The answer
was that Ant would, because the two men patched up their
friendship and their working relationship continued as usual.

The first meeting between the two women did not go well.
Ruth described Carole as having behaved like a mother super-
ior. Carole observed that Ruth spent the whole evening talking
to the men, and completely ignored her. At their second meeting
in the summer of 1954 Ruth, behaving rather like David,
squirted Carole with a soda siphon. By way of apology she then

gave Carole a 30-guinea christening gown for her new baby. Carole put it in a drawer and then gave it away.

Even in the fifties, racing cars took more capital than £7,000 to design and build, and soon David was running out of funds. His stepfather had heard that he was flashing his money around in the local pub, and so when David went to him for a loan, for the first time he refused. Now David began hanging round the Little Club making trouble—and Ruth began paying for him.

Maury Conley did not approve. Ruth stated in her proof of evidence that 'The proprietor of the club had started charging me a rental of £10 week for the flat because he knew David was living there and he had already warned me that he objected to it. He considered that it was bad for business.'

When David went away to Le Mans that same summer Ruth tried to break up with him by sleeping with another man, Desmond Cussen (see plate 9), but it didn't work. Around this same time David broke off his engagement. As Ruth explained in her proof of evidence:

> From then on he paid even more attention to me—he literally adored me—my hands, my eyes, everything except my peroxided hair which he always wanted brunette. Now he was free, I am afraid I allowed myself to become even more deeply in love with him. At that time … I trusted him implicitly. I still however did not think seriously of the possibility of marriage. I myself was still married and I believed … that his mother would never allow such a match.

The trust did not last. One night as David leaned over to turn off the light Ruth saw love bites on his neck and shoulders. She continued:

> I went cold with shock… he confessed he'd been with Faith Roberts—an usherette at the Prince of Wales theatre. He begged forgiveness … he began convincing me that our marriage was a possibility … and on the strength of this I approached my husband for a divorce. I said I was willing to let it go through undefended, claim no maintenance and allow my husband custody of my little girl. It was a measure of my love for David that I was prepared to give up my child of whom I was very fond.

And so the scene was set for tragedy. It involved an unbalanced, immature man who gave no consideration to anyone's feelings but his own, and thought he could do and say what he liked without consequence, and a woman from an impecunious and insecure background who was misguidedly willing to make greater and greater sacrifices for him. Both of them were prone to fits of violent jealousy, and both drank heavily. Cliff Davis commented: 'They were two people who should never have been allowed to meet because they reacted like dynamite to each other' (Hancock).

It was only a matter of time before the dynamite would explode.

THE FUSE IS LIT

In her proof of evidence Ruth showed that in many ways she was a realist when it came to David. After all, her experience of men had not led her to expect much from them:

> I realised that if he did get any money it would be spent on his racing car: but I did not mind this. I estimate that excluding rent, I was spending between £200–250 a year on David. In or about October 1954 he started becoming violent. He was constantly trying to belittle me in front of my guests and complaining that it was degrading to be associated with me because I ran a Club and generally trying to make me feel as if I was socially inferior to him … my nerves began to suffer … instead of cheerful and contented I was becoming moody and ill-tempered and this also was having an effect on the business. I also then started drinking more than I should have done.

Since David was no longer able to pay him, Ant Findlater took a job as a second-hand car salesman and could now only work on the prototype car in the evenings. David's dreams of building a winning sports car appeared to be turning to ashes.

Jackie Dyer, a Frenchwoman who was a barmaid at the Little Club and a close friend of Ruth's, was a witness to Ruth and David's relationship at this point. In a statement she gave on 1 July 1955 at Hampstead police station she had this to say of David:

He seemed to me to be a fool of a man who shouldn't go out with a girl like Ruth. He was very jealous of Ruth and was even jealous of me because she thought a lot of me. They quarrelled frequently and he beat and kicked her… she was frequently bruised about the body. (MEPO 2/9888)

She gave a statement to John Bickford on 9 July 1955 which was forwarded to the Home Office:

During the last six months prior to David Blakely's death both he and Ruth were drinking a very great deal of spirits.

Ruth Ellis would start drinking at 3 p.m. and go on to the small hours of the morning. She drank mainly gin and ginger and Pernod sometimes Champagne. I used to serve at the bar and on occasions when I saw she was drinking too much I used to give her water instead without her knowledge. I estimate that she would regularly drink half to a bottle of gin a day besides Pernod. She was not the kind to appear drunk, but I could tell when she was having too much because she used to get careless over the running of the business. She chain smoked at least 50 cigarettes a day.

Blakely often used to arrive intoxicated at 7 o'clock in the evening and go on drinking. In this condition he was quarrelsome and aggressive towards everyone. Ruth Ellis was not aggressive. There were, however, constant rows between them.

I remember on one occasion about a month before Christmas Blakely came into the Little Club about 8 p.m. in a bad temper. Ruth came back with Desmond [Cussen], having had some dinner with him. Blakely asked her where she'd been and she

said she had just had dinner with Desmond. He said, 'You're a
liar, you have been sleeping with him.' She said 'I am not a liar
and I do not like being called a liar—please go away.' He went
up to her and smacked her hard twice across the face. She was
sitting down. I went round the bar to get hold of Blakely and
she took hold of my hand and said 'No, let him alone' and took
him upstairs. I heard several thumps. She came back at 11
o'clock and said she was fed up and wanted to leave him. She
had been crying and was crying when she came back.

(HO 291/238)

Then Ruth left her job at the Little Club. It's not clear whether
she was fired or chose to leave, but Conley was a businessman
and the takings of the club had plummeted from £200 per week
to £70–£80. Ruth lost the flat she had been living in and a decent
source of income: her indulgence of David had cost her home
and livelihood. Managing the club had been a source not only
of income but also of great pride. Of this time she related in her
proof of evidence: 'I felt that if I did not have a rest, I would
have a break down. I thought that by leaving my flat David
would not be able to come and sleep with me and I thus might
find the strength to end the affair.'

It was now that Desmond Cussen came to the rescue. He,
like the Findlaters, was to play a crucial role in what happened
next.

RUTH'S ALTERNATIVE LOVER

In her proof of evidence Ruth described Cussen as being 'so restful compared to David'. He was certainly different from both George Ellis and David Blakely in one crucial respect: he never hit her. Cussen had been on the scene since 1952 and had first introduced Ruth to David. He was the director of his family business, a retail tobacco chain. On the face of it he was a more stable figure than the other men who had figured in Ruth's life up to this point. He was also a member of the Steering Wheel Club and on the fringes of the motor racing world.

Cussen suggested that Ruth move into his flat at Goodwood Court, Devonshire Street, just off Harley Street, and she did so on 7 December 1954, continuing to work at the Little Club until the New Year. The triangle was now in place. Cussen loved Ruth and had even offered to marry her. Ruth was infatuated with David, who was more in love with himself than anyone else. The break from the club, however, did not facilitate a break with David, as Ruth had hoped. They continued to sleep together, visiting the Rodney Hotel for the purpose 15 times between 18 December and 4 February. Ruth said in her proof of evidence: 'Although we quarrelled and he beat me, I just could not part from him.'

Cussen knew this, despite Ruth's lies, but he continued to play the good guy: he allowed Ruth to stay at his flat and paid her son's boarding school fees.

THE VIOLENCE ESCALATES

Christmas Day 1954 produced another violent row. David had been spending Christmas at his parents' house in Penn. Bored and drunk, he decided to drive up to town, intending to give Andre a toy gun. When he arrived at Goodwood Court, it was to find a note on the door giving the telephone number of a club Ruth was in, accompanied by friends including Cussen and Jackie Dyer. Andre was asleep inside the flat. David phoned the club and hurled abuse at her, calling her an unfit mother. Ruth rushed back to Goodwood Court to find him sulking in the doorway. Inside the row escalated. Ruth stated in her proof of evidence that 'He was drunk and unpleasant in front of my friends calling me a liar… he said in front of all our friends "I am a poor twisted boy and she's the one that's made me twisted. The girl I love sleeping with another man. It's her fault."'

Ruth accused David of sleeping with Carole Findlater. He denied this, suggesting that they go to the Findlaters' home in Tanza Road, Hampstead, and ask her. The couple (pursued by Cussen, who was worried about how drunk they were) drove off to Hampstead, only to find the house empty. The Findlaters were away for Christmas, but conveniently David had a key. Reconciled, he and Ruth spent the night there. Ruth later told Cussen she had had to spend the night with David because he had threatened to kill himself.

On New Year's Eve David humiliated Ruth further. He took

her for a drink in Penn, but on seeing his mother enter the Crown pub, left Ruth outside in the car and brought a drink out to her. Ruth must surely have wondered why he was suggesting marriage, if he couldn't even contemplate her meeting his mother.

By January 1955 both Ruth and David were saying the same thing to friends: that they wanted out of the relationship but the other one wouldn't allow it. This did not stop them both being acutely jealous of each other. Ruth, no longer working, had more time to obsess about David's actions. In her proof of evidence she stated that because of David's affair with Carole Findlater, 'I was not keen on his staying at Hampstead without me and I asked him not to... I did not like Carole very much because she was always running people down behind their backs.'

She was also convinced that David was having an affair with a woman in Penn. On 8 January 1955 they argued about this woman while at the Rodney Hotel; afterwards, David returned to Penn. When he didn't phone Ruth flew into a jealous rage. By the 10th she had phoned him at home and said that she was going to come down to Penn, confront the woman and tell David's mother all about it. She then sent him a telegram at work stating: 'Haven't you got the guts to say goodbye to my face—Ruth' (MEPO 2/9888).

David was frightened that she would cause a scene, or might even get some of her gangster friends to sort him out. On 14

January Ruth was granted her decree nisi; in three months there would be no impediment to her marrying David. Now she would discover if he was telling the truth when he said he wanted that to happen.

A quarrel on 4 February demonstrated how things were spiralling out of control. After a violent altercation at Desmond's flat, David phoned Ant Findlater and asked him to come and get him, saying feebly that Ruth had taken the keys to his car. When Findlater and his friend Clive Gunnell arrived, Ruth and David were very drunk and it was obvious a violent fight had occurred. Ruth was limping heavily and had a black eye. David also had a black eye, and told Ant that Ruth had tried to knife him; he showed him a long scratch on his arm. A fight ensued in the street when a hysterical Ruth tried to stop David leaving by sitting in his car and then taking the keys to Findlater's car. Eventually the two men managed to calm her down and take her off for a cup of coffee.

But things were far from over. That evening Ruth insisted that Cussen drive her out to Penn, where they arrived late at night. She hobbled to the door of David's flat and rang the bell. His nanny came to the door first, David appearing behind her in his pyjamas and dressing gown. On seeing Ruth David bolted out of the door, got into his car and drove away; eventually he returned and ran back into the flat before Ruth could stop him. This time no one would open the door to her.

Back in London, Cussen tried to persuade Ruth to go to

hospital, but she refused. The following morning she insisted on driving back to Penn to get an apology. En route they saw David's car outside the Bull, a public house at Gerrards Cross. Cussen parked the car and went inside. Mr Tovell, the cocktail bar attendant, gave a witness statement to the police on 14 April 1955 recounting what happened next: 'He [Cussen] went straight up to David, grabbed hold of his lapels, and said "Come on, you bastard, outside." David said nothing but went outside with the little man' (all witness statements from MEPO 2/9888).

Cussen frogmarched David outside, insisting he apologize to Ruth. David offered an apology of sorts, but it was not enough for Cussen, who suggested he try hitting him instead of a woman. David declined the offer. Ruth said she was going to go and talk to his mother. After David had driven off, Cussen persuaded her that talking to Mrs Cook would be foolish if she still wanted to marry David. They returned to London and Ruth went to the Middlesex Hospital to have her ankle X-rayed: it was badly bruised but not broken.

Later in the day a large bunch of red carnations—just as Clare had once sent—was delivered with a card saying: 'Sorry, darling, I love you, David' (HO 291/237).

That evening David said he had acted as he had because he couldn't stand Ruth living with Cussen. Ruth then spoke to Cussen, who said he would loan Ruth the money to set herself up in a flat with David. Ruth would keep the keys to Goodwood Court and cook for him. The following day she rented a room in

Egerton Gardens in Kensington. In a witness statement given on 19 April 1955, the landlady, Mrs Joan Winstanley, said: 'After taking the room she wanted the furniture changed round and borrowed a flower vase. She remarked that her husband Mr Ellis was very particular about having flowers in the room.' She went on to state that 'they appeared to be an average married couple'. However, 'Soon after they moved in a man whose name I discovered was Cussen used to call for Mrs Ellis at about 10am most working mornings after Mr Ellis had gone to work. I understood that he took her to a film studio where she worked as a model...'

As well as paying for Egerton Gardens, and Andre's boarding school fees, Cussen was paying for Ruth to take a three-week modelling course at the Margery Molineaux Agency, which finished on 29 March.

Ruth was also taking language lessons in her efforts at self-advancement. An interesting witness to her emotional state during this time was Marie Thérèse Harris, who tried to teach Ruth French between the end of January and the end of February. The lessons were not a success. In her witness statement given to the police on 16 April 1955 she said:

> Throughout my visits to her flat I found that Ruth Ellis was utterly unable to concentrate. I thought she was a good businesswoman but in my dealings with her she was very nervy and unsettled... I thought she looked like a person on the verge of a breakdown and had stopped work just in time.

It is easy to imagine that David was also frightened. Twice now Ruth had threatened to tell his family about his behaviour. She (like him) was becoming more violent and more jealous. Aided by Cussen, she continued to stalk him in Penn. At the end of February she spent a night outside the married woman's house, and caught David leaving in the morning. In the witness statement that this woman gave on 14 April 1955 she denied the affair and stated: 'At some point I can't remember when, David did tell me that the woman Ruth was violently in love with him, but he hated her guts. I was able to gather from all this that David was trying to shake off this woman but she would not be shaken off.'

Ruth then visited the woman and revealed her own relationship with David. In her witness statement the woman said: 'She left me in no doubt that there had been an association between herself and David… A little later she remarked, I thought in a peculiar way — "So young David is not having an affair in Penn." I replied: "As far as I know, he's not."'

Ruth was not convinced. In a detailed statement she gave to Bickford on 30 April 1955 she stated that Blakely admitted the affair:

> I asked David if he was in love with her. He said, 'No. I am in love with you'. I asked him what the attraction was. He said 'She's got something you haven't got, money'. I said, 'Yes, that is so important to you, isn't it?' I also said 'You get all I ever do get.' He said 'I know, I'm a rotter and I deserve all I get…

I shall have to marry you. I shall never be happy if I don't.'
> (quotes from HO 291/237)

They separated, but David wouldn't give up the keys to Egerton Gardens. After one week apart he was back, and said he had stopped the affair with the woman in Penn: 'I have been wanting to come home to you all the week, it's been hell. I have missed you so much. I have slept with you so long I cannot sleep without you.' However the following day, when Ruth and Cussen drove to Penn, there was David in the Crown having a drink with the same woman.

In March Ruth became pregnant. She claimed that the baby was David's, but Carole Findlater in her interview with Harry Ashbrook on 19 June 1955 stated: 'I felt she was telling a lie in order to establish a further hold on poor David. He was terrified of her and I don't believe he loved her. I think he hated her—and hated himself for having been involved with her' (HO 291/238).

Ruth described David's reaction in her proof of evidence: 'When he knew I was pregnant, he was at first very considerate about it and later changed and started saying nasty things such as "Well, all I can afford is about seven shillings per week."'

At the end of March there was another violent row. 'He then put his two fingers around my throat, with the other hand he punched me in the stomach... I said "You are mad, you are stark raving mad." He said "One of these days I will kill you." I said "You have done that already."'

The blow to the stomach led to Ruth having a miscarriage on 28 March. She said in her proof of evidence: 'David took no interest in my welfare... I was very hurt indeed about this and I began to feel a growing contempt for him.' Ruth blamed his attitude on the Findlaters. She continued to feel unwell until Tuesday 5 April.

This was the state of affairs when David Blakely began the last week of his life. Ruth had lost her job because of her infatuation with him, and was highly fragile emotionally. David had run out of money and was frightened by Ruth's threats to involve his family. Each of them was consumed with jealousy of the other. Each had tried to leave the other and failed. Both were drinking heavily and becoming increasingly violent. Jackie Dyer was in no doubt what she thought would happen. In a letter written to the Home Secretary on 25 June 1955, she stated about David: 'He had said to me, and to her in my presence. "If you leave me, Ruth, darling, I will kill you." I heard him say it so often. Their life together alternated between love and beating and he did the beating. He beat her unmercifully' (HO 291/236).

No one would have thought that the petite Ruth Ellis would be the one to do the killing.

CHAPTER TWO

'She's Got Him'

David had entered his car, the Emperor, in a race at Oulton Park in Cheshire on 2 April 1955. Ruth, still suffering from the effects of the miscarriage, went with him. When, on its practice run, the car broke down, he rounded on her, saying that she had jinxed him.

Back in London, over the next few days Ruth was ill with a temperature of 104 degrees from a cold she had caught in Cheshire. David was trying to raise money to get the car working; he even asked Ruth to request £400 from Cussen. Because it was the school holidays, Andre was staying at Egerton Gardens on a camp bed in the same room as David and Ruth. On the evening of Wednesday 6 April David came home early. Ruth later stated at the trial, 'He was quite happy, and he was saying everything would be alright, we would soon have some money, and talking about marriage again and all kinds of other little things' (trial quotes from HO 291/235). He handed her a photo of himself taken in preparation for Le Mans later that year; on it he wrote 'To Ruth, with all my love, David.'

On Thursday evening they went out to the cinema to see *Above Us, the Waves*. Ruth said at the trial, 'All through the cinema which was rather annoying, he was telling me he loved me and all kinds of things—and a very good film. He seemed very attentive to me.'

On the morning of 8 April, Good Friday, Blakely left Egerton Gardens saying that he was going to see Ant Findlater. Ruth thought that he would come and pick her up at 8 pm that evening and that they would spend the rest of the weekend together. She claimed that they parted on the very best of terms.

Jackie Dyer had phoned Ruth a week earlier and in a witness statement dated 1 July 1955 she related that 'She told me she was very happy and that she and David were going to get married.' But to the Findlaters, David was telling a completely different story. Ant Findlater stated this to the police on 10 April 1955:

> In the evening [Good Friday] we went to the Magdala Public House for a drink. Whilst we were there David said he had to get away about 8 to 8.30 to meet Ruth Ellis. My wife was with us. I suggested to him that this was foolish, continuing to see this woman, as he wanted to break with her. He said if I don't she will go to Penn again. I suggested he should stay with my wife and I for the weekend, that if she came along I would cope with her... one thing was obvious to me was that he was afraid to break with Ruth Ellis, this was chiefly because he was frightened of the trouble she would cause at Penn.

According to Hancock, during this conversation Carole said: 'For God's sake! Don't be so bloody spineless and silly. Any man can leave any woman. What can she do about it?'

Meanwhile Ruth was waiting for David to come and take her out. At 9.30 she phoned the Findlaters. The au pair answered the phone, telling her that the Findlaters weren't there and David wasn't with them. At 10.30 Ruth phoned again. This time Ant picked up the phone and said David wasn't there. Ruth kept phoning, becoming more and more exasperated. At first she had been worried, thinking David had done something stupid because he was depressed about his car. Now she felt humiliated and angry.

Cussen drove Ruth to Tanza Road. There she saw David's grey-green Vanguard parked near the Findlaters' house and realized she'd been lied to. She rang the bell. Getting no reply, she went to a telephone box and phoned. Someone hung up on her. Again she rang the doorbell. She thought she heard a woman giggling. Incensed and frustrated, she took a large rubber torch from Cussen's car and smashed three of the Vanguard's windows. At her trial she commented: 'I was in a rather nasty mood' (HO 291/235).

Ant Findlater phoned the police and then came out on to the street in his pyjamas. He told Ruth that David wasn't in his house. After more shouting, the police arrived at 2 am. In a witness statement given on 15 April 1955, Inspector Makin stated: 'I said to Mrs Ellis, "Did you cause this damage?" And she said, "Yes. This car is just as much mine as his. I have been living with him for two years. I shall stay here till I see him. I will pay for the damage."' He added: 'Mrs Ellis was behaving in a perfectly normal manner…'

Cussen drove Ruth back to Egerton Gardens. Of that evening, Ruth stated in her proof of evidence: 'I was beside myself with rage and humiliation. I remained awake in my flat all night, seething and brooding. I just could not believe, after all I had been through, that David could be such an unmitigated cad as to treat me as he had.'

At 8 am on the following day, Saturday 9 April, Ruth again phoned the Findlaters and again someone hung up on her. She took a taxi to Tanza Road, and waiting in a doorway saw David and Ant come out and look at the car. They then drove off. She suspected that they had gone to Clive Gunnell's garage to get the repairs done. When she phoned there and asked for Findlater, he again put the phone down on her. Cussen phoned and the same thing happened. Ruth spent that afternoon in Tanza Road spying on the Findlaters' home.

In the evening she returned to Egerton Gardens to give Andre his supper and put him to bed. Then back she went with Cussen to Tanza Road. Standing outside the house, she heard David's voice, and again giggling. She was convinced the Findlaters were using the au pair to lure David away from her. Later that night, when she saw the light of the living room under the Findlaters' flat go out, she thought that David was having sex with this girl, although in fact the au pair's room was at the rear and could not be seen from the street. Filled with a sense of injustice about his cowardly behaviour, Ruth was by now nursing powerful feelings of resentment and fury. These were fuelled by her inability to tell David how she felt.

As she explained in her proof of evidence, for a second night she stayed awake, brooding and drinking: 'I thought and thought. All kinds of things went through my head—all the things he had said to me and all he had done to me… I was raging inside.'

The following morning was Easter Sunday. At 9 am Ruth again phoned the Findlaters. When Ant picked up the phone she said: 'I hope you are having an enjoyable holiday because you have ruined mine.' Ant put the phone down on her again. That evening Ruth and Andre ate at Cussen's, then Cussen drove them home. Later he was to say to the police that this was the last he saw of Ruth that day. Of her mood in the early evening Ruth said at the trial: 'I was very upset. I had a peculiar feeling I wanted to kill him' (quotes from HO 291/235).

Meanwhile, a small party took place at Tanza Road that evening. Clive Gunnell was there, having supplied a gramophone and records. At 9 pm Carole ran out of cigarettes, and David and Clive drove the three-quarters of a mile to the Magdala pub (see plate 4) to buy some, and more beer.

David cashed a cheque for £5 with the landlord, Mr Colson, and the two men bought themselves a drink. Inside the pub, off duty, was PC Alan Thompson. He said in his witness statement of 10 April 1955: 'I saw a fair-haired woman wearing spectacles looking through the window of the saloon bar near the door. It was a ripple type glass but I could see the woman's face quite clearly as she was very close to the glass.' Ruth was prowling up and down outside the pub waiting for David.

The two men came out and David went to open the car. Ruth said, 'David,' and fired two shots. Clive Gunnell gave this account to the police on 10 April 1955:

> I heard David scream 'Clive' and I rushed round the back of the van and saw the woman Ruth with a gun in her hand. David was lying on the pavement face downwards and I saw her fire several more shots into David's back. I ran over and picked his head up and blood was spurting out of his mouth. David said nothing and I stood up.

George Stephen, a 16-year-old student, told the police, also on 10 April: 'All the time he was running, the woman was pursuing at a distance of about two yards and firing continuously… the woman was a platinum blonde and wore black rimmed glasses and a light costume.'

David James Lusty, an 18-year-old apprentice engineer, was also a witness and gave a statement on the same day. He saw David 'being chased by a woman'. Then, 'As the man lay on the ground the woman stood over him and fired two or three shots at him. She emptied the gun, as I heard two or three clicks from the gun after the last shot.'

Ruth had fired six shots, four into the body of David Blakely (see plate 7). In her proof of evidence she said:

> I remember standing there watching him in a completely detached sort of way—I did not feel anything except I seemed to be fascinated by the blood—I have never seen so much blood. He seemed to gasp two or three times, heaved and relaxed. I think that must have been when he died. I saw his outstretched arm—his watch and signet ring. I was rooted to the spot—I neither moved nor spoke… I had a curious feeling of relief.

Clive rushed back into the pub and said, 'She's got him.'

One of the shots had ricocheted off the pavement and hit a woman called Mrs Gladys Kensington Yule in the thumb. She and her husband got in a cab, and after a short argument because the taxi driver did not want her bleeding all over his seats, they were driven to Hampstead General Hospital. There she was told that she had suffered a fracture of the first metacarpal bone and that she would probably experience permanent stiffness in her right thumb.

PC Alan Thompson had heard the noise and gone outside: 'The woman said, "Phone the police". I went up to her and said I am a police officer and at the same time took the gun away from her.' Ruth made absolutely no attempt to run away or disguise what she had done.

David was rushed to New End Hospital. On the journey Mr Pett, an ambulance man, saw something poking out just below his lowest rib; it was a bullet. He removed it and later handed it back to the police. David was announced dead on arrival at the hospital by Dr Elizabeth Beattie. His body was removed to Hampstead Public Mortuary, where Ant Findlater identified it at 2.30 pm the following day. Meanwhile, Ruth had been taken to Hampstead police station.

'THIS UNPLEASANTNESS'

At the police station Ruth's property was confiscated, including her signet ring, which 'had been bent all shapes due to the fights I had had with David'. An hour and a half later three CID officers, Detective Superintendent Leonard Crawford, Detective Chief Inspector Leslie Davies and Detective Inspector Peter Gill, came to see her. Crawford told her he had viewed the dead body of David Blakely at the mortuary and said 'I understand you know something about it.' Ruth was asked if she had anything to say. This is the statement she gave (see plate 5):

> I have been cautioned that I am not obliged to say anything unless I wish to do so, and that anything I do say will be taken down in writing and may be given in evidence.
> (Signed) Ruth Ellis
> I understand what has been said. I am guilty. I am rather confused.
> About two years ago I met David Blakely when I was manageress of the Little Club, Knightsbridge. My flat was above that.

I had known him for about a fortnight when he started living with me and has done so continuously until last year, when he went away for about three weeks, motor racing. He came back to me and remained living with me until Good Friday morning.

He left me and promised to be back by 8 pm to take me out. I waited until half past nine and he had not phoned, although he always had done in the past. I was rather worried at that stage as he had had trouble with his racing car and had been drinking.

I rang some friends of his named Findlater at Hampstead, but they told me he was not there. I was speaking to Findlater, and I asked if David was all right. He laughed and said: 'Oh yes, he's all right.' I did not believe he was not there, and I took a taxi to Hampstead, where I saw David's car outside Findlater's flat at 28 Tanza Road. I then telephoned from nearby, and when my voice was recognized they hung up on me.

I went to the flat and continually rang the doorbell, but they would not answer. I became very furious and went to David's car, which was still standing there, and pushed in three of the side windows. The noise I made must have aroused the Findlaters, as the police came along and spoke to me. Mr Findlater came out of his flat, and the police also spoke to him.

David did not come home on Saturday, and at nine o'clock this morning [Sunday] I phoned the Findlaters again, and Mr Findlater answered. I said to him: 'I hope you are having an enjoyable holiday' and was about to say: 'because you have ruined mine', and he banged the receiver down.

I waited all day today for David to phone, but he did not do so. About eight o'clock this evening I put my son Andria to bed.

I then took a gun which was given to me about three years ago
in the club by a man whose name I do not remember. It was
security for money, but I accepted it as a curiosity. I did not
know it was loaded when it was given to me, but I knew next
morning when I looked at it. When I put the gun in my bag I
intended to find David and shoot him.

I took a taxi to Tanza Road, and as I arrived, David's car
drove away from the Findlaters' address. I dismissed the taxi
and walked back down the road to the nearest pub, where I saw
David's car outside. I waited outside until he came out with a
friend I know as Clive. David went out his door to open it. I was
a little way away from him. He turned and saw me and then
turned away from me, and I took the gun from my bag and I
shot him. He turned around and ran a few steps around the car.
I thought I had missed him, so I fired again. He was still
running, and I fired the third shot. I don't remember firing any
more but I must have done. I remember he was lying on the
footway and I was standing beside him. He was bleeding badly
and it seemed ages before an ambulance came.

I remember a man came up, and I said: 'Will you call the
police and an ambulance?' he said: 'I am a policeman.' I said:
'Please take this gun and arrest me.'

This statement has been read over to me, and it is true.

(HO 291/235)

Ruth Ellis gave this statement within three hours of killing her
lover. It is clear that she had already made up her mind that she
should die. With the phrase: 'When I put the gun in my bag I
intended to find David and shoot him,' she condemned herself

out of her own mouth. On the day before she was hanged, however, she was to give another statement that contradicted the contents of this first one in certain crucial respects.

On Easter Monday a post-mortem was carried out on David's body by Dr Albert Hunt, lecturer in the Department of Forensic Medicine at the London Hospital Medical College. He gave a statement on 12 April 1955 describing how one bullet had entered the lower part of David's back: 'The track passes through the muscle and abdominal cavity, through the second part of the duodenum, through the lower part of the liver and out through an oval wound just below the rib.' A second bullet had produced an

> entry wound below the angle of the left shoulder blade... the track passes between the ninth and tenth rib upwards piercing the lung and passing out of the chest cavity in front of the spine, through the aorta and across the trachea and up the right side of the neck. The bullet is lying in the deep muscle of the right side of the tongue.

Another wound was just above the outer part of the left hip bone, penetrating the skin and fat only, with an exit wound quite close by. There was also a shallow mark on the inner side of the left forearm. Hunt's conclusion was: 'Two bullet wounds in the body entering through the back, one almost horizontal to the ground, the other passing sharply upwards with the bullet still in the body. These have caused death from <u>Shock</u> and <u>Haemorrhage</u> due to gun shot wounds' (quotes from MEPO 2/9888).

DCI Davies returned to Hampstead police station and
informed Ruth that she would be charged with murdering
David. She was cautioned twice more and in reply to the final
charge said: 'Thanks.' She was then taken to Hampstead Magistrates' Court, which had been specially convened because it was
a bank holiday, and there was remanded in custody to appear in
the same court on 20 April 1955. There was a brief reference to
the court appearance on the BBC six o'clock news and some
stories in the provincial papers, but none in the national newspapers which were on strike.

PRISONER 9656

At Holloway prison Ruth requested that a Bible and a photo of
David be sent to her. In the hospital case papers (PCOM 9/2084)
there is a description by the prison doctor of his first encounter
with Ruth. He described her as 'a heavily made up woman with
platinum hair ... rather hard-faced and abrupt in manner ...
very co-operative to examination'. He went on: 'There is an
almost complete absence of display of emotion, but she is obviously very tense ... and trying hard to be matter of fact.' When
asked if she had previous convictions, he wrote, 'she appears
shocked by the suggestion'.

One of the first things Ruth did was write a letter to David's
mother, Mrs Cook, on 12 April 1955. There is a copy in MEPO
2/9888; the errors are Ruth's own:

Dear Mrs Cook

No dought these last few days have been a shock to you.

Please try to believe me, when I say, how deeply sorry I am to have caused you this unpleasantness. No dought you will hear all kinds of stories regarding David and I. Please do forgive him for deceiving you, has regarding myself. David and I have spent many happy times together.

Thursday 7th April, David arrived home at 7.15pm, he gave me the latest photograph he had, a few days hence had taken, he told me he had given you one.

Friday morning at 10 o'clock he left and promised to return at 8 o'clock, but never did. The two people I blame for David's death, and my own, are the Findlayters. No dought you will not understand this but <u>perhaps</u> before I hang you will know what I mean. Please excuse my writing, but the pen is shocking. I implore you to try to forgive David for living with me, but we were very much in love with one and other unfortunately David was not satisfied with one woman in his life.

I have forgiven David, I only wish I could have found it in my heart to have forgiven when he was alive.

Once again, I say I am very sorry to have caused you this misery and heartache. I shall die loving your son. And you should feel content that his death has been repaid.

Goodbye

Ruth Ellis.

The tone of the letter is startling. The phrase 'this unpleasantness' suggests a woman apologizing for a slight argument, rather than for shooting dead a mother's son. Perhaps it can be read as the letter of a woman numb with shock and holding at bay the emotional reality of what she has done. One thing seems very clear: Ruth appeared to be in no doubt that she was going to hang. This is also what she said to her solicitor, John Bickford of Cardew-Smith and Ross.

Bickford had been contacted by Duggie Howell, the star crime reporter of the *Daily Mirror*. According to a memorandum in HO 291/238 dated 21 February 1956, Howell had taken Joan Winstanley, Ruth's landlady, out for a drink at the Bunch of Grapes in Brompton Road and suggested that she write to Ruth recommending Bickford, who the paper would then pay for. Mrs Winstanley wrote the letter and Bickford went to Holloway to introduce himself to Ruth. He then contacted Leon Simmons, a senior legal executive at Ruth's civil solicitors Victor Mishcon, and asked if there was any objection to him handling Ruth's case—there was no objection. It is clear that despite the press strike the newspapers were sniffing around the case, eager to have the inside track on what they knew would be a sensational story.

At his first meeting with Ruth, Bickford asked if there was anything he could do for her. She asked him to go to her mother and collect her belongings, and hold them. Then she told him to pass a message to Cussen, saying that she had told the police that the gun had been given to her as security for a loan. Bickford did as she asked. In a statement given many years later on 11 June 1972 he relates what happened next:

> I returned to see Mrs Ellis the following day… she told me she
> thought she was guilty and just wanted to get the whole thing
> over with, so that she could die and join David Blakely. I talked
> about her responsibility to her children and so on, and urged
> her to make an effort. She made it quite plain that she was
> quite prepared to die; but wanted her story told so that her
> friends and relatives would know why she had done what she
> did. (MEPO 26/145)

Even though there was no doubt that Ruth had shot David, this
did not inevitably mean she had to hang. Elizabeth Tuttle in
her book *The Crusade Against Capital Punishment in Great
Britain* gives the following statistics for the years 1946–55. Of
573 men put on trial for murder, 286 were sentenced to death
but only 133 were actually executed. The statistics for women
were 144 put on trial, 20 sentenced to death and only 4 executed.
Many of those tried were the beneficiaries of what Jonathan
Goodman and Patrick Pringle in their book *The Trial of Ruth
Ellis* term 'perverse jury verdicts'. In cases where they thought
the death penalty would be too severe, juries often sought to
find 'reasonable doubt' where in fact it did not exist, and would
return verdicts of guilty but insane or guilty of manslaughter.
Even if the defendant was convicted of murder, there was still
the chance that he or she might be reprieved on the advice of
the Home Secretary, who did not have to justify his decision.
So there were grounds for hope. The key as far as Bickford was
concerned was whether sufficient sympathy for Ruth could be

generated for the jury to give a recommendation of mercy.

In prison Ruth was giving the authorities no problems. The hospital case papers show that she was a model prisoner (see plate 10). The following extracts are taken from the notes:

> 17.4.55 Has been quietly reading most of the day. Makes no complaint
> 19.4.55 Slept well. Very composed
> 20.4.55 Appears very indifferent in attitude
> 22.4.55 Reading most of the evening. Very talkative and bright when visited, appeared rather strained

THE POLICE INVESTIGATION

The police, meanwhile, were interviewing witnesses and putting their case together. On 25 April 1955 Lewis Charles Nickolls of the Metropolitan Police Laboratory, New Scotland Yard, wrote the following report concerning the murder weapon:

> On receipt the Smith and Wesson revolver was in working order... the trigger pull is 9½–10lbs uncocked, and 3lbs cocked... the cylinder contained, on receipt, 6 spent cartridges. In order to fire these 6 cartridges it is necessary to cock the trigger 6 times, as in the case of a revolver pulling the trigger only fires one shot. To pull a trigger of 10lbs requires a definite and deliberate muscular effort. (this and following quotes from MEPO 2/9888)

It was a deliberate effort that Ruth Ellis had made six times.

The police did not believe her story about how she obtained

1 The high life: Ruth Ellis with an unidentified friend in 1954. The setting is probably the Little Club in Knightsbridge, which Ruth managed.

2 *Above*: David Blakely (1929–55).

3 *Right*: Ruth and David in celebratory mode after one of his motor races, from the *Daily Herald*, 12 July 1955. (HO 291/237)

4 *Below*: The Magdala pub in Hampstead where Ruth Ellis shot David Blakely on the evening of 10 April 1955. (HO 291/237)

CHAMPAGNE FROM PAPER CUPS

David Blakely had been placed second in a race. Ruth Ellis ran to him, with a bottle of champagne. "He kissed me in front of everyone," she says. " The champagne foamed over the car. David shouted: 'What a christening, darling!' We drank out of paper cups."

Continuation of Statement of ... *Ruth Ellis (Mrs)*

car outside. I waited outside until he came out with a friend I know as Clive. David went to his car door to open it. I was a little way away from him. He turned and saw me and then turned away from me and I took the gun from my bag and I shot him. He turned round and ran a few steps round the car. I thought I had missed him so I fired again. He was still running and I fired the third shot. I don't remember firing any more but I must have done. I remember then he was lying on the footway and I was standing beside him. He was bleeding badly and it seemed ages before an ambulance came. I remember a man came up and I said, "Will you call the police and an ambulance?" He said "I am a Police man." I said, "Please take this gun and arrest me." This statement has been read over to me and it is true. *Ruth Ellis*

Statement written down and read over by Pete Gill Detective Inspector "S" in the presence of Det. Supt Crawford and Det Chief Inspector Davies

Signature ....

witnessed by ....

Use both sides if necessary. (If this is done, *both* sides of the form must be signed and witnessed).
M.P.-51917/30,000 Apr./1954 G28 (4)

5 Page from Ruth Ellis's police statement of 11 April 1955. (MEPO 2/9888)

6 *Above*: Police photograph of Blakely's car, retrieved from the murder scene. (HO 291/237)

7 *Right*: One of several crime scene sketches, showing the location of Blakely's bullet wounds. (MEPO 2/9888)

8 *Opposite*: The police list of Blakely's possessions, which range from amyl nitrate to a toy whistle. (MEPO 2/9888)

PAGE 3.

TWO PAIRS OF DRIVING GOGGLES.
ONE PAIR OF SUNGLASSES.
ONE DYNAMO TYPE TORCH.
ONE PAIR OF SOFT LEATHER BLACK LACE-UP TYPE BOOTS.
ONE PAIR OF GREY SOCKS.
ONE GREEN JERSEY.
ONE PAIR GREEN JERSEY WITH BADGE ON BREAST POCKET.
ONE PAIR OF BLACK TRACK SUIT TROUSERS.
ONE CREAM COLOURED SLEEVELESS PULLOVER.
ONE CLOTH HELMET.
ONE RED SCARF.
ONE BOTTLE CONTAINING A COLOURLESS FLUID.
ONE TIN CONTAINING CAR POLISH.
ONE TIE.
ONE WOOLLEN CAR RUG.
ONE PEN KNIFE.
ONE PAIR OF LEATHER MITTENS.
TWO PAIRS OF GLOVES.

METROPOLITAN   POLICE.
* * * * * * * * *   *** * * * * ***

HAMPSTEAD STATION,

"S" DIVISION.

PROPERTY OF THE LATE DAVID MOFFAT DRUMMOND BLAKELY NOW IN

POSSESSION OF POLICE.

ONE "STANDARD VANGUARD" MOTOR VAN, INDEX NO. O.P.H. 615.
FOUR £1 BANK OF ENGLAND NOTES.
EIGHT SHILLINGS AND SIXPENCE SILVER.
THREEPENCE BRONZE.
ONE CHEQUE BOOK ON THE NATIONAL PROVINCIAL BANK, BEACONSFIELD,
CONTAINING THREE CHEQUES, NOS. 924210 TO 924212.
TWENTY THREE KEYS.
THREE KEY RINGS.
ONE BIRO PEN.
ONE PETROL LIGHTER.
ONE METAL TOY WHISTLE.
ONE BOX CONTAINING CAPSULES OF AMYL NITRATE.
ONE PAIR OF SUN GLASSES.
ONE LEATHER CASE CONTAINING A COMB AND A METAL NAIL FILE.
ONE PLASTIC CLOTHES PEG WITH SAFETY PIN ATTACHED.
SIX PACKETS OF "WHIZZ BANGS".
ONE LOG BOOK RELATIVE TO STANDARD MOTOR VAN, INDEX NO. O.P.H. 615.
ONE CERTIFICATE OF INSURANCE No. CV 5455997 RELATIVE TO STANDARD
MOTOR VAN, INDEX No. O.P.H. 615.
ONE LOG BOOK RELATIVE TO MOTOR CAR, INDEX No. H.L.O. 168
ONE CERTIFICATE OF INSURANCE No. P.M. (1) 544

Mrs. Ruth Ellis and Mr. Desmond Cussen photographed at the Little Club, in Knightsbridge, where, he told the court, he often met her.

9 *Above*: Ruth with Desmond Cussen, from the *Daily Sketch*, 29 April 1955. (HO 291/237)

10 *Opposite*: Page from Ruth's hospital case papers documenting her cheerful and cooperative behaviour, although she is 'very upset about children's future', 9–12 June 1955. (PCOM 9/2084)

11 *Opposite top*: Ruth Ellis's signature giving formal permission for her hair to be dyed for her trial, 17 June 1955. (PCOM 9/2084)

1955	Treatment, including Prescriptions	History and Progress of Case
9-6-55	Night Report Unchanged, slept from (approx) 11 pm until 6 A.M. Had lad breakfast.	
	Ting Pot Chlor od x2 Head cold KClV AK ℥i bd	
	X 2 Continue Tonnough bd 2 bymylling	
9.6.55	Day Report - Is very distressed at times today quietly reading most of the time. Still has heavy cold. Looks very pale and languid resting most of the day. Is very upset about children's future says she regrets that she went be here to see them grow up. Spent evening sitting by her bed playing patience. Has a heavy cold + looks poorly.	
10-6-55	Night Report. Unchanged, no definite complaints. Slept at intervals. Had lad breakfast.	
10.6.55	Day Report - Is fairly cheerful today but looks poorly. Still has heavy cold though it is a little better. Spent most of the day quietly reading in bed.	
	Evening Report. Satisfactory evening reading most of the time. Supper taken.	
11-6-55	Night Report. Patient is unchanged, slept well had breakfast. No definite complaints.	
11.6.55	Day Report - Remains fairly cheerful and outwardly calm. Sitting quietly in bed reading most of the time. Still has heavy cold and looks rather poorly.	
11. 6.55	Evening Report. Quietly reading most of the evening. Has no conflict. John Suffin.	
12.6.55	Day Report - Fairly cheerful and still outwardly calm. Cold is subsiding butyet looks rather poorly still. Is very talkative when visited ; quietly reading in bed most of the time	
12.6.55	Weight 102 lbs.	

and moral point of view I feel I ought to die - "An eye for an eye and a tooth for a tooth". I am sorry for what I did in so far as it affects other people: but not so far as it affects myself and David. I am sure he really did love me: but it was the interference of other people that caused all the trouble.

My great mistake was when I went to live at Desmond's flat - that gave the Findlaters a weapon with which to work on David and I am sure they were urging him to break with me. It accounts for all that business with the Nanny - David had become so weak where women were concerned. He used not to be when I first met him, I think the fact that he was hard to get in the first place, was part of his attraction to me when he originally started coming to the Little Club.

I have given in detail the whole history of my association with David and, as I feel now, after full consideration, all I want is that my Counsel should see to it that I can tell my story.

I know the penalty for what I have done and I am willing to pay it. As I am now I would not have done it: but, as I was then, with circumstances as they were, I cannot help feeling that it was inevitable.

Ruth Ellis

Amended 17. 6. 55 and re-signed

23.

12 *Above*: Extract from Ruth Ellis's proof of evidence, blaming 'the interference of other people that caused all the trouble'. (HO 291/237)

13 *Right*: Ruth and David with the Findlaters, from the *Woman's Sunday Mirror*, 3 July 1955. (HO 291/237)

the gun. On 16 April Marie Thérèse Harris had come forward
with information about guns, and gave a witness statement. She
talked about being let into Goodwood Court by Andre:

> I chatted with the little boy and mentioned that we were
> troubled by pigeons. He said what you want is a gun, and with
> that he opened the drawer of the table on which I was writing.
> In the drawer I noticed among other things, two guns which at
> first I thought were his toys. He handled one, the larger one,
> then said 'It's all right, it's not loaded.' Then he put it back and
> closed the drawer.

DCI Davies and DC Claiden went to Cussen and asked him
about this. Having denied giving Ruth the revolver, he opened
the drawer and handed them a starting pistol and a Webley air
pistol. Mrs Harris identified the guns as being the ones she'd
seen, but the police never showed her the murder weapon.

The air pistol was passed to Lewis Nickolls, who reported
on 20 April 1955: 'The oil [on the Smith and Wesson] is a mineral
oil. It is similar to the oil on the Webley air pistol, but it is not
possible to say whether they are the same oils.'

The police were also looking into the fact that Blakely had
had two capsules of amyl nitrate in his pocket. They interviewed
his doctor, Dr MacGregor, on 16 April 1955. MacGregor stated
that 'I have never at any time given him capsules of amyl
nitrate.' Nickolls explained that the drug was used 'in cases of
heart disease to cause dilation of the veins and also in the relief
of asthma'. But Blakely was suffering from neither of these; he

was probably using the amyl nitrate as a sexual stimulant.

On 22 April Davies submitted his report on the case together
with 26 witness statements to the Assistant Commissioner, 'C'
Department (the CID) and thence to the Director of Public
Prosecutions:

> In spite of what Cussen says that Ellis wanted to be rid of
> Blakely and he would not leave, the weight of evidence points
> quite clearly to the position being completely reversed. The two
> people concerned Blakely and Ellis are of completely different
> stations in life… this girl has tried to rise above her humble
> beginnings and is considered by her parents to have done very
> well for herself. However they both agree that their daughter
> always had a violent temper. On meeting Blakely and realising
> that his class was much above her own, and finding he was suffi-
> ciently interested in her to live with her and, if we are to believe
> Cussen, to promise her marriage, it seems she was prepared to
> go to any lengths to keep him. Finding this impossible she
> appears to have wreaked her vengeance upon him.

Davies's opinion demonstrates how rigidly class conscious the
1950s were. After all, Ruth Ellis had been supporting Blakely
and had been beaten by him, so surely those were good enough
reasons for her wanting to leave him. What stopped her was not
that he was middle class and therefore a 'good catch', but the
fact that she was in love with him and in the grip of a destructive sexual obsession.

Davies had this to say about the gun: 'Efforts are being

made to trace from whom Mrs Ellis obtained the revolver used by her in this offence, but so far without success. Inquiries are being continued with this end in view because I found it difficult to believe her story…'

Davies also said in the report that the driver of the taxi Ruth had claimed to have taken on the night of the murder had never been traced. This was odd because the police had an established routine for making enquiries among London cabbies. A long journey from Kensington to Hampstead on Easter Sunday (not a busy time for taxis) with a delivery point very close to the site of a widely publicized murder would surely have stuck in the mind of a cabbie, especially when the fare was a striking blonde. If Ruth hadn't taken a cab, then how had she got to Hampstead? And, more to the point, who had driven her?

Ruth's second appearance at Hampstead Magistrates' Court on 20 April had led to another week-long remand in custody. On 24 April she wrote the following letter to Clive Gunnell:

Dear Clive

Thanks for your letter. No dought [sic] you have been shocked rather badly.

Thanks for all the racing news, it is nice hearing all about Peter and the rest. How is the girlfriend, you know who I mean.

Give my best regards to all the people I know, who are <u>still</u> my friends.

Well at least Clive, you can say, I told you so. You have been right all the time.

Holloway is a jolly nice place better than Butlins holiday
camp you are always talking about peace and quiet.

Everyone is jolly nice here it has surprised me.

... I have no (faulse (I have forgotten how to spell) idears
about my position, so do not worry (friend) I shall be able to
take it.

Please excuse the writing paper, heading but the printer
could not get my own crest printed in time.

Well, Clive, I am in court Hampstead police station? On the
28th Thursday, so you will be reading more about things, so
don't forget to order your copy right away.

Bye for now, Clive. Thanks once again.

R Ellis (PCOM 9/2084)

At the next hearing on 28 April the main police witnesses were
called, and the press was there in force. On the 29th the *Daily
Sketch* gave the following report under the headline 'Blonde
model for trial accused of shooting race driver':

> Ellis in a grey and black tweed costume, toyed ceaselessly with
> an embroidered handkerchief ... she propped her black suede
> shoes against the railings of the cage-like dock of the tiny
> panelled court ... when she saw the photo of Blakely her light-
> grey eyes narrowed. (PCOM 9/2084)

The next day the papers went to town. These headlines come
from press cuttings in prison file PCOM 9/2084: 'Court hears of
loves of the "Little Club" girl' (*Daily Express*); 'Model shot car
ace in the back, say police' (*Daily Telegraph*); 'Four Bullets As

He Lay Dying' (*Daily Mail*); and 'Hostess with two lovers shot one' (*Daily Herald*).

On 11 May Ruth appeared in the Central Criminal Court of the Old Bailey. This was so that Mr Melford Stevenson QC, who was to be her counsel at the trial, could ask for the case to be held over to the next session because the defence was not complete.

Peter Rawlinson (one of the barristers who represented Ruth at her trial) visited her in the cells of the Old Bailey on the occasion when the trial date was set. He recounts what happened in his book *A Price Too High*:

> 'You will make certain, won't you,' she said quietly, 'that I shall
> be hanged. That is the only way that I can join him.' I caught
> my breath and said that she must not talk like that. But she
> repeated, 'I want to join him. I want to join him.'

Not surprisingly the strain of waiting to go on trial took its toll on Ruth. The 23 May entry in her hospital case papers reads: 'Played "Patience" most of the morning. Says she finds that reading doesn't help any more. Is beginning to find concentration difficult' (this and following quotes from PCOM 9/2084).

During this time her mental health was being assessed. An ECG on 3 May showed 'nothing to suggest either the presence of organic brain disorder or of epilepsy'. An independent psychiatrist, Dr Dalzell, examined Ruth twice and sent a report to the Director of Public Prosecutions on 13 June. It said that:

She gave no history of any previous mental illness or nervous trouble and no history of violent behaviour, uncontrolled outbursts of temper, or undue aggression. She stated she felt 'tired and run down' that she had a cold and a two month miscarriage ten days previously. She stated that after having shot David Blakely she felt no regret, and considered that she was justified in having done what she did because of the way in which he had treated her, and she still felt so justified... In my opinion she knew the nature of the act which she performed and knew it was wrong.

Bickford had not been informed of Dalzell's visits, and wrote a ferocious letter to the prison governor about the matter. He was later to hotly dispute the assertion that Ruth 'still felt so justified'. But Dr Penrys Williams, the Holloway doctor, had come to the same conclusion as Dalzell—that Ruth was sane and fit to plead.

On 4 June Bickford had sent the defence's psychiatrist, Dr Duncan Whittaker, to visit Ruth at Holloway. Whittaker had concluded that she was mentally stable. However he claimed that she was emotionally immature, because a mature woman would have been prevented from doing what she did by thoughts of her children.

Ruth had obviously not given any of the psychiatrists an accurate description of her abusive first marriage. Marks and van den Bergh quote Dr Rees's colleague Dr William Sargant as saying that Dr Rees was very surprised not to be called as a defence witness at the trial. He would have been able to give a clearer picture of Ruth's mental history than Dr Whittaker. Maybe Ruth was ashamed and did not want to admit to the true nature of her first marriage, taking pills or being the patient of a psychiatrist. Maybe she was determined to die. What is abundantly clear is that she was not offering excuses, nor looking for sympathy.

As the date of the trial approached Stevenson was searching in vain for a precedent that would enable him to put forward a defence based on 'provocation by jealousy'. As the English law stood none existed.

On 13 June the hospital case papers include the following report on Ruth: 'Upset, on return from solicitors visit had been crying. Said she had insisted on seeing the photographs of "David" [presumably those of his corpse]. They were worse than she'd imagined. States it is the first time she has cried since she has been here.'

But Ruth had not lost her spirit. On 15 June she wrote to a friend:

> Dear Alex,
>   I am writing to you, again, because I hate the thought of you, being without money. Perhaps you can get <u>another</u> £5 for this letter, like you got for the last one.
>   Yes, Alex, I still have a sense of humor [sic]
>   Goodbye
>   R Ellis

It's always nice to know, Alex, at times like this, who's [sic]
one's friends are.

Two days later something of a rather more frivolous nature
was causing her concern. She begged the governor, Dr Charity
Taylor, to allow her to dye her hair. The governor sought
approval from the Home Office, and Ruth was allowed a full
peroxide rinse (see plate 11). The hospital case papers contain
references to this:

> 18.6.55 Very cheerful and chatty during the morning. Discussed
> the clothes she is to wear to court—also wondering if her hair
> is going to look nice. She says she used to get her hair bleached
> twice a week in a hairdressers as her hair grew so fast.
>
> 19.6.55 Bleaching of her hair appears satisfactory. Prisoner
> says quite good but could rinsing have made her hair a little too
> blue?

Bickford in his brief to counsel related that:

> Efforts have been made to enable the accused to have her hair
> attended to because it is now changing colour patchily as a
> result of continued neglect... it is submitted that it is of consid-
> erable importance to the Accused that she be able to look her
> best at the trial. (HO 291/237)

Also important to Ruth was that the whole story should be
presented in court, especially the part played by the Findlaters,
whom she held responsible for David's death.

She was to be bitterly disappointed.

CHAPTER THREE

Blonde in the Dock

On 20 June 1955 the trial began in Number One Court of the Old Bailey. Popular stage shows at the time were *Salad Days*, *Kismet* and *The Boy Friend*. Ruth's trial was to prove just as much of an attraction, if not more. Members of the public needed a ticket to gain access and the touts were doing the same sort of business they had done at the trials of John Christie, almost exactly a year before, and of Christopher Craig and Derek Bentley in December 1952. Some punters were said to have paid £30 for a seat.

The proceedings were to last one and a half days, a startlingly short period of time. A full trial transcript is included in HO 291/235, from which all quotations are taken.

THE LAW

The presiding judge at the trial was Mr Justice Havers. Ruth's defence team was made up of Melford Stevenson QC, Sebag Shaw and Peter Rawlinson. Stevenson had little experience of criminal courts, having specialized until now mainly in divorce. His lack of experience was to be particularly critical when he came to question Ruth Ellis herself—and she had not given him an easy job.

In 1955 there was no legal concept of 'diminished responsibility'. This was only introduced in the Homicide Act of 1957, partly in response to the Ellis case. As the law stood there were four possible defences to a charge of murder: (1) proving that the defendant did not commit the act; (2) proving the defendant was insane when the act was committed; (3) proving the defendant acted in self-defence; and finally (4) establishing that there was sufficient provocation to lead the jury to reduce the charge from murder to manslaughter.

It was clear that Ruth Ellis had shot David Blakely and had not acted in self-defence, so that left insanity and provocation. Insanity was covered by the McNaughten Rules. To succeed, the defence had to prove that the person committing the crime was suffering from such a defect of reason or disease of the mind that they did not know the nature and quality of the act they were carrying out, or did not know it was wrong. (An example is the person who thinks he is squeezing an orange only to find he has his hands round someone's throat and is strangling them.) But insanity had already been ruled out as a defence: Ruth would not agree to it, and all the medical reports stated that she was fit to plead. That left provocation as the only possible defence.

Provocation was defined by case law as an act or acts which would cause in a reasonable person 'a sudden and temporary loss of self-control, rendering the accused so subject to passion as to make him or her not master of his mind'. (An example is the man who comes home and sees his wife in bed with another man, and 'in the heat of the moment' picks up a knife and stabs one or both of them.) The provocation, however, had to take place very close to the act of murder for the defence to succeed, and this was the problem for Ruth's defence team.

Nowadays the concept of cumulative or 'slow burn provocation' is recognized by common law, providing a defence for battered women who have been subjected to persistent and serious violence by their partners. But in 1955 this was not so. The fact that David had assaulted Ruth ten days to two weeks before the murder (Ellis couldn't remember the exact date) was not relevant in law.

Ruth took her place in the dock dressed in a two-piece suit with an astrakhan collar and a white blouse. Her hair was immaculate and platinum blonde. She looked like a sexually confident woman. She did not look cowed or broken, she did not look contrite. It was clear she was not embracing the role of a remorseful, downtrodden victim. The blonde hair that was so important to her was to prove highly detrimental. 'Blonde tart' is exactly what someone said loudly in the public gallery shortly after she entered the dock.

It is worth remembering that the 1950s was the era in which

Doris Day flourished. The war had been a time of unparalleled sexual and social freedom for many women. But its end saw a backlash: women were being told firmly that their place was in the home as wife and mother. Ruth Ellis was no Doris Day. She was a working-class divorcee with two children by two different fathers; she had worked as a hostess and managed a night club. She was having an affair with two men at the same time. With the double standards of the period, no stones were cast at the middle-class David Blakely for frequenting the clubs, but a great many were cast at Ruth for working in one. Her defence was going to have to work very hard to break through the prejudices of the time and present her in a sympathetic light.

THE PROSECUTION

Ruth pleaded not guilty and a jury consisting of ten men and two women was sworn in. The prosecution was led by Mr Christmas Humphreys, Senior Prosecuting Counsel at the Old Bailey (and paradoxically a founding president of the Buddhist Society). His previous 'successful' prosecutions had included those of Timothy Evans and Craig and Bentley.

After laying out the facts of the case he said:

> In a word the story which you are going to hear outlined is this, that in 1954 and 1955 she was having simultaneous love affairs with two men, one of whom was the deceased and the other a man called Cussen, whom I shall call before you. It would seem

that Blakely, the deceased man, was trying to break off the connection. It would seem that the accused woman was angry at the thought that he should leave her, even although she had another lover at the time. She therefore took a gun which she knew to be fully loaded which she put in her bag. She says in a statement which she signed: 'When I put the gun in my bag I intended to find David and shoot him.' She found David and she shot him by emptying that revolver at him...

The prosecution then called its first witnesses: PC Banyard, who had made a plan of the scene of the shooting; DC MacMacken, who had photographed the corpse; and Mrs Winstanley, Ruth's landlady, who gave evidence that Ruth and David had shared the same bed.

Now Desmond Cussen entered the witness box. He was very pale and small beads of sweat could be seen running down the side of his face. He confirmed what Humphreys had said in his opening statement about his relationship with Ruth and his part in driving her back and forth to Hampstead during the bank holiday. When Humphreys came to the day of the murder Cussen reiterated what he had told the police in his witness statement: he had spent the day with Ruth and her son and had driven her back to Egerton Gardens at around 7.30, and that was the last he saw of Ruth on that day.

Stevenson was to cross-examine only two of the prosecution's 16 witnesses. Cussen was the first. The whole of the cross-examination is reproduced below:

Q: You have told the jury that you and this young woman were lovers for a short time in June, 1954. Is that right?

A: Yes.

Q: And that was a time when Blakely was away, was it not—at the Le Mans race in France?

A: Yes.

Q: Were you very much in love with this young woman?

A: I was terribly fond of her at the time, yes.

Q: Did she tell you from time to time that she would like to get away from Blakely, but could not, or words to that effect?

A: Yes.

Q: And at that time did she repeatedly go back to him?

A: Yes.

Q: At a time when you were begging her to marry you if she could?

A: Yes.

Q: Have you ever seen any marks or bruises on her?

A: Yes.

Q: How often?

A: On several occasions.

Q: How recently before Easter had you seen marks of that kind?

A: On one occasion when I was taking her to a dance.

Q: When was that?

A: The 25th of February.

The Judge: Of this year?

A: Yes, my Lord.

The Judge: 'When I was taking her to a dance'?

A: Yes.

Q: Did you help to disguise bruises on her shoulders?

A: Yes.

Q: Were they bad bruises?

A: Yes, and they required quite heavy make-up too.

Q: I do not want to press you for details but how often have you seen that sort of mark on her?

A: It must be on half a dozen occasions.

Q: Did you on one occasion take her to the Middlesex hospital?

A: Yes, I did.

Q: Why was that?

A: She came back when she was staying at my flat, and when I arrived back I found her in a very bad condition.

Q: In what respect?

A: She had definitely been very badly bruised all over the body.

Q: Did she receive treatment for that condition at Middlesex hospital?

A: Yes.

And that was it. Cussen's story had not been challenged. He had not been asked about what he had done during the day of the murder. He had not been asked about the gun. He had not been asked if he taught Ruth to fire it. He had not been asked if he drove her to Tanza Road on the evening of the murder.

Interviewed by Marks and van den Bergh, Mr Justice Havers later said that he, like the police, never believed Ruth's version of where she got the gun from, and could not rule out that it was given to her by Cussen. But the defence didn't raise the matter and therefore he could do nothing. Bickford in his statement of 11 June 1972 explained that they had purposely decided not to pursue the matter of the gun:

> If evidence had been available that she had been acting in concert with someone else … her chance of an alternative verdict of manslaughter, on the possible grounds of lack of premeditation, were virtually nil and, likewise, her then very feasible chance of a reprieve would virtually have vanished.
>
> (MEPO 26/145)

It is also true to say that the defence was not helped by Ruth, who was refusing at this stage to implicate Cussen in any way. Tellingly, this was the last time he saw her. Up until the trial he had visited her in prison, bringing her items like make-up and chocolates. After the trial all contact ceased.

Ant Findlater was the next prosecution witness. As far as Ruth was concerned, the Findlaters had been largely responsible for what had happened. She wanted to see them exposed and humiliated in court. The prosecution's examination was short, covering the fact that David had wanted to leave Ruth and the events over the Easter weekend.

Stevenson now had the opportunity to cross-examine. After jumping around in a confusing manner with his questions, he decided to ask Findlater about Ruth's state of mind during the call that preceded her damage to the car.

Q: Was it quite plain when you spoke to her on the telephone that she was in a desperate state of emotion?

A: No.

Q: What?

A: I said no.

Q: Do you mean she was quite calm? Do you really mean that?

A: It was just a telephone conversation. She rang me up, as she had done hundreds of times, and asked if I knew where David was. It was just a telephone conversation.

Q: I know it was just a telephone conversation. Just bear in mind what she said and the way she said it and the fact that she afterwards pushed out those windows. Did you observe no indication of her being a very desperate woman at that time?

A: No.

Q: Never mind about the word desperate. Was it obvious to you that she was in a state of considerable emotional disturbance?

A: Well, I did not get that impression over the phone. She might have been.

The one question Ruth wanted Findlater to be asked was whether he and his wife had deliberately dangled their nanny in front of David to lure him away from her—and Stevenson failed to ask this. She also wanted Carole Findlater to be questioned. But although Carole had been subpoenaed, the defence had decided that calling her would not help Ruth's case.

Next came Clive Gunnell, who confirmed his involvement in

the incident when he and Findlater came to fetch David after his row with Ruth, and the details of the shooting.

Lewis Nickolls, director of the Metropolitan Police Laboratory, then testified that the gun taken from Ruth was the same gun from which the shots that killed David had been fired. The most sensational part of his evidence came at the end of his questioning:

> Q: Can you help us at all as to the distance from the body at which one of the bullets had been fired in respect of the wounds found in the body?
>
> A: Yes. I examined the clothing of the deceased man and I found that on the left shoulder at the back of the jacket there was a bullet hole. This had been fired at a distance of less than three inches.
>
> [This not surprisingly produced a number of controlled whistles in the court.]
>
> Judge Havers: Why do you say that?
>
> A: That is because of the circle of powder fouling round the hole. The others are all fired from a distance.

Two more witnesses were examined by the prosecution: PC Thompson and Mrs Gladys Yule. The latter said that Ruth had chased David round the car after firing at him. Further witnesses said that David had been dead on arrival at New End Hospital. Dr Hunt explained how the bullets had killed him and DC Claiden told how he had taken possession of the bullets removed from the body.

The final witness for the prosecution was DCI Davies. He stated that when Ruth gave her statement, despite saying that she was 'very confused', she 'seemed very composed'. The defence asked no questions of any of these last witnesses.

In John Bickford's opinion, this reticence in cross-examination was to prove significant. In a statement sent to the Home Office dated 28 June 1955 (HO 291/237), supporting Ruth's plea for a reprieve, he gave the view that 'The whole explanation for her attitude in court lies in my view in the fact that Findlater was not seriously cross-examined.' This was a crucial factor in demoralizing Ruth and affecting how she presented herself in court. Stevenson's reasoning had been that cross-examination might be interpreted as mud-slinging and not create a good impression. Bickford further stated that

> Mr Melford Stevenson decided on Monday morning just before the trial that he would subject the witnesses of the prosecution to the minimum of cross-examination… this had two effects, one … the trial moved at such speed that Mrs Ellis was in the witness box before I could explain to her the decision had been made…

The second effect was that Ruth went into the witness box 'disheartened and somewhat bewildered'.

THE DEFENCE

Stevenson now opened the defence. Having made clear that the decision not to challenge the prosecution case had been deliberate, he moved on to outline his intended approach:

> One of the ingredients in that offence [murder] is what lawyers call malice… if a person finding themselves in the position this unhappy young woman now is, has been the subject of such emotional disturbance operating upon her mind so as for the time being to unseat her judgment, to inhibit and cut off those censors which ordinarily control our conduct, then it is open to you, the Jury … to say that the offence of which she is guilty is not the offence of murder, but the offence of manslaughter, and that, members of the Jury, is what we, on her behalf, ask you to do in this case.

He went on to highlight a crucial element in his defence:

> It is always an unpleasant thing to say anything disagreeable about someone who is dead, but I venture to think the story she will unfold to you can leave no doubt in your minds that he [Blakely] was a most unpleasant person…
>
> You may take the view that there really is no doubt that this young woman was driven by the suffering she endured at the hands of this man to do what she did, and it so operated on her mind that her judgment for the time being was unseated, her understanding was gone, and that malice, which is an essential ingredient in the offence of murder, was absent in this case…

Members of the Jury, that will depend upon the view you take of this girl when you see her here in the witness box... never before as far as I know ... has any court had to consider a case in which the defence rely upon jealousy, and the state of mind in which a woman gets when a man to whom she is devoted behaved as this one did, as constituting this defence of provocation.

Stevenson had made it clear that the impression Ruth made as a witness was very important. Now, her high heels clicking on the floor of the court room, she walked from the dock into the witness box. This was Stevenson's opportunity to present what had happened from her point of view. But to do that he would have to lay bare the emotions which had led to her killing her lover.

Helena Kennedy in her book *Eve Was Framed* gives an interesting insight into the way this could have worked:

Taking a defendant through the evidence may seem like a straightforward process to the onlooker, but there is a special skill involved in choreographing a witness's account so that, while coherent, it also gives the jury a sense of the misery and turmoil that can lead to behaviour that would normally never even be contemplated. The counsel's task is to enable the client to communicate their sense of desperation, or whatever other aspects of their emotional state figured in the offence. It should be like watching a *pas de deux* and the parties must be in step... Expressing such emotion in a court of law, particularly

> Court One at the Old Bailey, is a daunting prospect and is
> usually only possible if the person on trial has established a
> degree of trust and understanding with their counsel.

The truth was that no such trust existed between Ruth and
Stevenson.

RUTH IN THE WITNESS BOX

By any judgement what happened next was a disaster for Ruth
Ellis. It could of course be argued that she had decided to throw
her life away and that there was nothing that Stevenson could
have done. A less charitable point of view might be that Stevenson's lack of empathy and experience led to him bungling his
examination of Ruth very badly indeed.

Ruth's dejection and indifference to the outcome of the
proceedings was obvious from the start. As Bickford said in his
statement to the Home Office of 28 June 1955, 'she grossly
understated her case ... she gave her evidence almost wilfully
badly ... she tended to exculpate Blakely as regards the various
assaults' (HO 291/237). Her answers were curt and at times she
was inaudible even to the judge. She did nothing to counter the
view that she was a cold-hearted 'tart', who had shot her lover
and was now showing a callous indifference to what she had
done. She talked about her abortion in a casual manner,
describing her unborn child as 'a mess', and said she could not
even remember the date on which David first proposed—yet

this was a proposal from a man whom Stevenson had described in his opening speech as being 'one of her fundamental requirements'.

Ruth said of David, 'He was a very likeable person and I got very attached to him.' This was hardly an accurate description of the destructive passion that fuelled their love–hate relationship. Even on the question of his violence she was muted:

> Q: How did the violence manifest itself?
> A: He only used to hit me with his fists and hands, but I
> bruise very easily, and I was full of bruises on many occasions.

Kennedy has this to say of the way Ruth dealt with the violence: 'Like many battered women before and since, her reduction of his violence was probably a coping mechanism, and it also displayed the complicated emotions that go with loving someone who treats you like a dog.'

In general Ruth's responses were unemotional and matter-of-fact, and Stevenson seemed incapable of drawing her out in a manner that might have demonstrated her humanity or her vulnerability. The defence's approach was that jealousy had unseated her reason, but Ruth appeared in her answers to be thoroughly rational and collected. On being asked about her feelings on seeing David leave the woman in Penn's house, she said:

> I was obviously jealous of him now. I mean the tables had been
> turned. I was jealous of him, whereas he, before, had been
> jealous of me. I had now given up my business—what he had

wanted me to do—left all my friends behind and connected
with clubs and things, and it was my turn to be jealous of him.

She did not even express any emotion when describing her
miscarriage:

> Q: In March did you find that you were pregnant?
> A: Yes.
> Q: At the end of March did you do anything about that preg-
> nancy? What happened about it?
> A: Well, we had a fight a few days previously—I forget the
> exact time—and David got very, very violent. I do not know
> whether that caused the miscarriage or not, but he did thump
> me in the tummy.
> Q: And that was followed by a miscarriage?
> A: Yes.

At only one point did Ruth show any emotion; it was when she
was handed the photograph of David which he had signed and
given to her on the Thursday before the bank holiday. She
looked at it and began to cry. Stevenson asked that she be
allowed to sit down but she refused.

If this had softened her image then what she was to say later
did exactly the opposite. Stevenson took her up to the day of the
murder and the point where she was about to set off for Tanza
Road. Then Ruth said: 'I had the peculiar idea I wanted to kill
him.' Obviously startled, Stevenson replied: 'You had what?'
Ruth repeated: 'I had an idea I wanted to kill him.'

In response to the question: 'Why did you do it?', she replied:

14 Ruth Ellis's parents, Bertha and Arthur Hornby, going to visit her in Holloway, from the *Sunday Dispatch*, 3 July 1955. (HO 291/237)

Outside The Jail

RUT

Ruth Ellis's father and mother pictured at the gates of Holloway Prison when they went to visit her yesterday.

TREAT OFFICIALLY

4 JUL 1955

To;   Sunday.

His Honour,   Cheltenham.

The Home Secretary

London.

H.O. REGISTRY

- 4 JUL 1955

FROM P.S.

SIR,

    Ruth Ellis received justice at the hands of a British judge and jury. She killed a man and was sentenced to death. A just verdict.

    In your hands, Sir, lies the almost divine power to add mercy to justice. I write to ask you to exercise it for the following reasons which I will endeavour to put before you.

    Hers, I believe, was not a planned crime of malice aforethought. Though she appeared to carry it out with cool deliberation and determination, she was, I believe, under the stress of an overpowering emotion which swept her completely off balance and deprived her temporarily of normal reasoning.

    This was not so much jealousy as the terrible black misery which floods the heart of a woman when her love, her real 'homing' love, is betrayed. Betrayed, not so much physically, as mentally, the instinctive trust she has placed in the man chosen of her heart.

    There is a natural instinct in a woman's mating which is different to a man's. Apart from the social obligations of religion and convention a man's natural instinct is to go when he is satiated. Apart from physical desire there is no compelling instinct in mating for him. But for the woman, mating, especially with a man who has somehow suited her so that he has won her love, arouses a fundamental natural instinct, which for the want of a better word, I will call the 'homing' ix instinct. It is connected with the maternal instinct to make an abiding place for her children.

    When this love and trust is given to a man, even by a woman of apparently light and sophisticated character, and is repudiated and betrayed by that man, there is an over- whelmingly strong sense of monstrous outrage and injury. This sense of injury is akin the feeling expressed in the words:
    'Had it been an enemy who had done this thing unto me, but it was thou, mine own familiar friend!'
    I believe that it was this tremendous sense of out-

15 One of the many letters sympathetic to Ruth Ellis received by the Home Office, from 'A woman of the Public', Cheltenham, 4 July 1955 (HO 291/235)

16 *Below*: Contrasting letter, also from a woman, reminding Lloyd-George of the stark facts of the case, 10 July 1955. (HO 291/236)

17 *Right*: Gwilym Lloyd-George in 1951, just a few years before he made his decision on Ruth's fate.

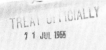

TREAT OFFICIALLY
7 1 JUL 1955

Dear Sir

Will you forgive my saying that the majority of women do <u>not</u> join in the hysterical clamour to reprieve Ruth Ellis?

I have been asked by many to represent their point of view in this matter.

While grieving that any criminal should have to suffer the extreme penalty of the law, we see no reason in this instance for evading that law on any pretext whatsoever.

Ruth Ellis was guilty of <u>murder, pre-meditated, deliberate and cold-blooded</u>. There was not even the extenuating circumstance of distracted love, for she had not been faithful to the man she murdered.

If she is reprieved it creates a precedent whereby every prostitute who thinks herself slighted by a former lover will think herself entitled to butcher him.

Yours faithfully

a. mils. Stirling

July 10

H.O. REGISTRY
1955
FROM P.S.

Reference____CCS 600/1

I have given the most careful and anxious consideration
to this case.

As I conceive my duty, it is to review all the circumstances of a capital case in order to see if there are such
mitigating circumstances as would justify me in recommending
interference with the due course of law.   It is no part of
the duty of a Home Secretary to give any weight to his own
approval, or detestation, of the penalty prescribed by law;
and least of all is it his duty to alter the law merely on
the grounds that he thinks that a penalty which is appropriate
for a man is inappropriate for a woman.

There may be circumstances in a capital case where
special considerations apply to a woman which would not be
applicable in the case of a man.   A recent example is the
case of Mrs. Sarah Lloyd.   I can find no such special
circumstances, however, in the present case.   The crime was
a premeditated one and was carried out with deliberation.
The prisoner has expressed no remorse.   I can find nothing
to justify my taking a less serious view of this case than of
other similar cases where the crime was of a callous and
calculated nature.

I have been pressed from many quarters to exercise
clemency in this case on the grounds of the prisoner's sex and
of her yielding to jealousy which is alleged by some people
to be stronger in the case of a woman than in the case of a
man.   But our law takes no special account of the so-called
crime passionel, and I am not prepared to differentiate
between the sexes on the grounds that one sex is more
susceptible to jealousy than the other.

Cases may arise from time to time where a husband deserts
a wife, or a wife deserts a husband, or where one spouse is
deceived by the other spouse in the most provocative circumstances, and clemency may be appropriate in such a case.
In the present instance, there is no such element; and the
woman was as unfaithful to her lover as he was to her.

I have consulted the trial Judge and discussed all the
details of the case with him.   He told me that he was unable
to suggest any mitigating circumstances, and although he
naturally disowned any responsibility for the ultimate
decision, he said that he himself could find no sufficient
grounds for suggesting that clemency would be appropriate.

If a reprieve were granted in this case, I think that
we should have seriously to consider whether capital punishment
should be retained as a penalty.

The fact that many people have signed letters and
petitions on behalf of the prisoner is a factor to which I have
given due weight.   I do not think that it is a conclusive
factor.

After much anxious thought I have come to the conclusion
that this is a case in which the law should be allowed to
take its course.

18 *Left*: The Home Secretary's reasons for turning down Ruth Ellis's appeal, 11 July 1955. (HO 291/235)

19 *Below*: Last-minute telegram from Frank Owen, a *Daily Express* journalist, 12 July 1955. (HO 291/238)

20 *Right*: Jackie Dyer (left) visiting Holloway on the day of the execution, 13 July 1955.

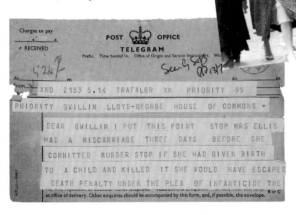

POST OFFICE
TELEGRAM

XND 2183 5.14 TRAFALGR XN PRIORITY 99

PRIORITY GWILLIM LLOYD-GEORGE HOUSE OF COMMONS =

DEAR GWILLIM I PUT THIS POINT STOP MRS ELLIS
HAD A MISCARRIAGE THREE DAYS BEFORE SHE
COMMITTED MURDER STOP IF SHE HAD GIVEN BIRTH
TO A CHILD AND KILLED IT SHE WOULD HAVE ESCAPED
DEATH PENALTY UNDER THE PLEA OF INFANTICIDE THE

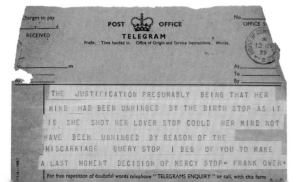

POST OFFICE
TELEGRAM

THE JUSTIFICATION PRESUMABLY BEING THAT HER
MIND HAD BEEN UNHINGED BY THE BIRTH STOP AS IT
IS SHE SHOT HER LOVER STOP COULD HER MIND NOT
HAVE BEEN UNHINGED BY REASON OF THE
MISCARRIAGE QUERY STOP I BEG OF YOU TO MAKE
A LAST MOMENT DECISION OF MERCY STOP= FRANK OWEN+

21 *Above*: Crowds outside Holloway Prison for the execution of what was to be the last woman hanged in England, 13 July 1955.

22 *Right*: The coroner's inquisition on Ruth Ellis's death. (HO 291/238)

23 *Opposite*: Page from John Bickford's statement implicating Desmond Cussen, 11 June 1972. (MEPO 26/125)

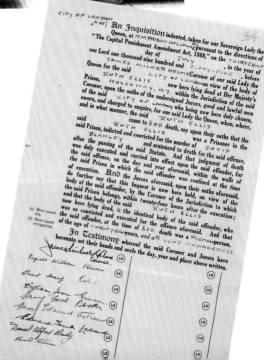

much as anybody of the association and was quite clearly
on the side of Ruth Ellis. So much that, having been
assured by me that I only had Ruth Ellis' interests at
heart, he told me of the part which he had played in
the affair.

12.   Amongst other things, he told me that he had
supplied her with the revolver. He said that he had
cleaned and oiled it. He wiped the bullets and loaded
it. He showed her how it worked, his explanation being
that she knew that he had a collection of three or four
guns, she was so beside herself and so persistent and he
was so much in love with her that he, eventually, gave way.

14.   Throughout Good Friday and Saturday, she had been
in constant touch with him and he had driven her wherever
she wished to go, in search of Blakely.

15.   She was quite beside herself with grief, jealousy,
frustration and, consequently, anger. From recollection
and without reference to papers, I feel sure he told me
that it was on Easter Sunday morning at his flat that he
prepared and gave her the gun.

16.   Probably about mid-day or in the early afternoon,
Mrs. Ellis and Cussens, together with her young son
Andrew, or "Andy" as she called him, aged then between
10 and 13, I can check this if necessary, drove to Penn
Buckinghamshire in search of Blakely. They did not find
him and started off on the return journey. On the way
back, I think near Gerrards Cross, they stopped by a wood
and Ruth Ellis got out of the car and fired at a tree.
It is just possible that the son may recollect this. They
continued on their way and when going over one of the
bridges over the Thames, I am not at the moment certain
which one he said it was, Cussens stopped the car and
having previously re-loaded the gun with another bullet
to replace the one which had been fired, he threw the
remaining spare bullets and the cleaning materials, which
he had used, into the Thames.

17.   They drove back to Mrs. Ellis' flat in Egerton
Gardens and I seem to recollect that he said he left her
there with the boy. Whether he waited or not, I cannot
now say; but she put Andy to bed, took the gun in her

VOICE FROM THE DEAD

On tape— Ruth Ellis's prophetic love song

A TAPE - RECORDING unique in the history of murder trials has been handed to Scotland Yard.

It was made by Ruth Ellis, who was hanged 18 years ago, her victim, David Blakely, and Mr. X, the man who was his rival for Ruth's love and helped her to prepare the crime.

Mr. John Bickford, the solicitor who acted for Ruth Ellis, received the tape from Mr. X. Until now its existence and contents have remained undisclosed.

By LAURIE MANIFOLD, HARRY WARSCHAUER and ALAN HIDOUT

It is understood that Mr. X, one of several men in her life, provided the tape-recorder for use as a novelty during various Christmas festivities in which Ruth took part.

It was used first to record the chatter at a party.

Ruth is heard introducing herself as "Ruth Ellis," and she asks her 13-year-old son to give a "Merry Christmas" message. Others at the tape

recorded party were Mr. X and David Blakely.

Both Ruth and David Blakely are heard describing how they have spent the previous day, and there is some argument between them.

Blakely calls Ruth "a liar," while she tells him:

"I must say you look very nice, anyway."

Blakely's reply is indicated by his reply: "I've been looking this way all day, darling."

The second part of the tape records a conversation at a later date between Ruth and Mr. X.

Ruth Ellis. For the first time, the voice of a woman who was hanged.

David Blakely, Ruth's victim. His song of her love.

obviously in an intimate situation.

It must have been recorded with Ruth's knowledge, because she announces the date

"Don't you know that David's a little bastard?" Ruth asks Mr. X.

Mr. X: Darling — you know him better than I do.

Ruth: When he said he left me I really believed it. I should have known better.

Ruth then breaks into song.

Answer me, oh my love, Just what am I to do? Please answer me, oh Lord.

Tell me how I come to lose my love. Please answer me, oh Lord.

HAGGARD

"I think that's nice," Ruth comments, and then resumes her song.

He was mine yesterday, I believed that love was here to stay. Tell me, tell me, where I've gone astray. Please answer me, oh Lord.

If he's happier without me—

Ruth again talks of Blakely, the playboy who refuses to leave her and whom she will soon shoot down.

"I wonder if he still cares ... He's such a bastard... really, you know.

"I think I've been a fool. I was living with him only for 18 months. Can you imagine it."

Mr. X:—God. Was it as long as all that? No wonder you're looking haggard, dear....

Ruth:—Oh, shut up or you'll have a black eye. David gave me a black eye, sitting in a car park on New Year's night....

I'm so glad it's over and done with anyway. He's just a little drip. He's a cheap skate. I think he'd **** anything don't you!

Mr. X:—I shouldn't worry about it darling.

Ruth:—I'm not worrying about it really. I shall spit at him across the room one day. Or throw a soda syphon all over him. I don't care. I shall go to bed early tonight—

Mr. X: Not with him though.

Ruth, with a laugh: Yes, darling. More, More. More. More. More. More.

water all over him and make him look silly.

She has lowest of the low. Just a little skunk. Rotten to the core.

Anybody can have him as far as I'm concerned. He's just a drip. Have he has the nerve to call himself the social life of Buckinghamshire I wouldn't know.

At this point Ruth starts to sing again.

I will believe we were meant for each other ...

Mr. X: Just go to sleep darling.

Ruth: Oh, shut up. I don't want to go to sleep yet.

MORE ...

Mr X: You want more, do you?

Ruth, with a laugh: Yes, darling. More, More, More, More, More.

There is a pause, then Ruth speaks of giving up her "sleeping-powders" with Blakely.

Mr. X: No. You mean now there's no one else to keep him and pay the rent for him.

Ruth: Yes. (She laughs). You're being naughty now.

Mr. X: Who — me? Well, aren't I being truthful?

Ruth: Of course.

The song Answer Me is reproduced by kind permission of Bourne Music, Ltd., of London. Ruth Ellis's version differs slightly from the original lyric.

A phone call could have saved her

A LOCAL telephone call could have saved the life of Ruth Ellis, the last woman to be hanged in Britain.

That is the tragedy revealed by the Sunday People's inquiry into one of the most notorious murder cases of the century.

On the eve of her execution 18 years ago, Ruth confessed that a man had given her the loaded murder gun, and driven her to a point near the spot where she killed her faithless lover, David Blakely.

If that confession had been confirmed, it would have utterly changed the picture painted of Ruth Ellis at her trial as a lone, pitiless avenger. A full investigation would have

been launched into the part played in the murder by that other man, Mr. X, and Ruth Ellis would have been reprieved.

Her death-cell statement was rushed to the Home Office. But neither officials there, nor the police, sought confirmation from the one person who could have given it, apart from Mr. X. himself.

Confession

Mr. John George Arscott Bickford, Ruth Ellis's solicitor at her trial, would have fully corroborated Ruth Ellis's statement.

For Mr. X had confessed his

part in the crime to Mr. Bickford, even admitting he had shown Ruth how to use the gun.

The solicitor had been unable to use the evidence at the time, or even afterwards. Ruth Ellis herself had begged him to suppress it.

But Mr. Bickford was ready to disclose it on the eve of the execution date—if he had been asked. He wasn't.

Last week Mr. Bickford, now 61 and his hair silver-grey, said in a voice bitter with regret:

"The Home Office did not contact me. The police did not come near me.

"Yet I possessed the evidence they were seeking as the hours were running out for

Ruth Ellis. Neither the Home Office nor the police told Mr. Bickford that Ruth had at last confessed to the truth. Mr. Bickford, released him from his duty to keep silent. "One 'phone call from the Home Office would have been enough to release me from my bond of confidence.

Missed

"I could have given them the facts that would have saved Ruth Ellis. I will regret to my dying day that I did not. . . ."

The police did try to check out Ruth's death-cell statement —

At 4.30 p.m. on the day before the execution two detectives—an inspector and a detective constable — were detailed to investigate Mr. X.

The two detectives missed their quarry as his alibi by a narrow margin — he had left to minister before they arrived.

They rushed to his home—to find that he had been seen leaving with his solicitor.

The detectives maintained their vigil until what they call "late in the evening," when they were instructed to withdraw by a Deputy Commander at Scotland Yard.

Ruth Ellis was hanged early next morning

"THE TRIAL OF RUTH ELLIS," edited by Jonathan Goodman and Patrick Pringle, will be published in the "Celebrated Trials Series" by David & Charles Ltd. early in 1974.

24 The *Sunday People* article reporting Ruth's last statement, 9 December 1973. (MEPO 26/145)

'I do not really know, quite seriously. I was just very upset.' This reply even startled the judge, who asked her to repeat what she had said.

Mr Humphreys now stood up for what was to be an extremely short cross-examination:

> Q: Mrs Ellis, when you fired that revolver at close range into the body of David Blakely, what did you intend to do?
> A: It is obvious that when I shot him I intended to kill him.

And with that Ruth returned to the dock. She had in effect signed her own death warrant. The intense emotions that had led her to kill David—her anger, jealousy and fear arising from the abuse, exploitation and rejection dealt by her lover, and the humiliation she felt at being kept at arm's length by the Findlaters—had clearly been laid out in the proof of evidence she gave to Bickford as part of his preparation for the trial. But in court these had not been explored in any depth. Any defence based on provocation needed to reveal how utterly the relationship had battered Ruth, both physically and emotionally. Without that the defence made no sense.

Nor had there been any attempt to deal with the 'heat of the moment' aspect of provocation. Obviously this was tricky because Ruth had said that she had taken the gun and travelled to Hampstead with the intention of killing David. But questions put to her could have revealed whether her intentions had varied at different times. For example she could have been asked how she felt when she saw David come out of the pub, and how he had responded when she called his name. Did he ignore her? Had his response to her in that instant 'provoked' a sudden temporary loss of self-control?

The next witness was Dr Duncan Whittaker. His rather dubious claim was that women were more prone to hysterical reactions than men. Stevenson asked: 'And under the influence of these hysterical reactions what becomes of their standards of conduct and control?' To which Whittaker replied: 'They are inclined to lose some of their inhibitory capacity and solve their problems on a more primitive level.'

In cross-examination Humphreys cut to the chase:

> Q: In your view at the time of the killing she was mentally capable of forming the intent to kill?
> A: Yes.
> Q: In your view was she at the time within the meaning of the English law, sane or insane?
> A: Sane.

And with that a miserable defence came to an end.

Mr Justice Havers then dismissed the jury and began a lengthy discussion with Stevenson about the law in relation to provocation. Stevenson wanted the judge to allow the jury to decide whether Ellis was guilty of manslaughter, rather than murder, on the basis of provocation. He argued David's actions had provoked Ruth to such a state of jealousy that she lost control. This provoked the exclamation from the judge: 'But this is new law.' Summing up what he thought Stevenson was arguing, he made it sound preposterous:

> Does your proposition come to this, putting it in its simplest form: if a man associates with a woman, and he then leaves her suddenly, and does not communicate with her, and she is a jealous woman, emotionally disturbed, and goes out and shoots him, that is sufficient ground for the jury to reduce the crime of murder to manslaughter?

Understandably, Stevenson could not give a straight answer. As the English law stood in 1955 there was nothing which admitted the defence of *crime passionel*.

The court adjourned until the following day, which began with the jury absent and the judge making a judicial ruling to the barristers on both sides:

> I feel constrained to rule that there is not sufficient material even on a view of the evidence most favourable to the accused for a reasonable jury to form the view that a reasonable person so provoked could be driven, through the transport of passion and loss of self-control, to the degree and method and continuance of violence which produced the death and consequently it is my duty as a judge and as a matter of law, to direct the jury that the evidence in this case does not support a verdict of manslaughter on the grounds of provocation.

All that was left for the jury to decide was whether Ruth had murdered David or not. Stevenson accepted that there was no point in making any closing speech for the defence. The judge called the jury back in and summed up.

The proceedings then rushed to their inevitable conclusion. At 11.52 am the jury retired. Twenty-three minutes later they reached their verdict: Ruth was found guilty. When asked if there was anything she wanted to say, she declined. Mr Justice Havers placed the traditional black cap on his head and condemned her to death. As he finished, almost simultaneously Ruth said, 'Thanks' and the chaplain said, 'Amen.'

The jury had added no recommendation for mercy.

What is one to make of this trial? One approach might be that Ruth Ellis was let down by her lawyers. However the documents in the National Archives (HO 291/237) show that John Bickford worked hard on the case and did his job thoroughly. Ruth's proof of evidence reveals all the conflicting emotions she was gripped by during that bank holiday weekend and the volatile nature of her relationship with Blakely. There are also briefs to counsel, supplementary briefs to counsel and a long list of mitigating circumstances. Yet virtually none of this came out in court.

It is tempting to see Melford Stevenson as the villain of the piece: he was after all in charge of the trial strategy and later became the sort of 'hang 'em and flog 'em' judge who invites casting in that role. It is arguable, however, that his strategy was a perfectly reasonable one. Ruth Ellis *had* killed Blakely and Blakely was the murder victim. His decision to go easy on the prosecution witnesses because he wanted to avoid alienating the sympathies of the jury was not without merit. Yet to prove provocation Stevenson had to lay bare the provoking behaviour. To do this he was relying on Ruth to reveal how Blakely's behaviour had driven her to do what she did—but when she entered the witness box she refused to dance in step. The result was certainly no *pas de deux*. Maybe his strategy would have worked if Ruth had been more cooperative and if he had had more experience in the conducting of murder trials; a greater degree of empathy with his client might also have helped. As it was his questions produced more and more disastrous responses.

Ruth Ellis now had 21 days left to live. Would she do anything to save herself? Would she tell the truth of what had happened on the day she murdered David Blakely? Or would she take that secret to the grave?

CHAPTER FOUR

An Eye for an Eye

The next three weeks of Ruth Ellis's life were lived out in the condemned cell at Holloway. It was a double one, 15 feet wide and 14 feet deep and decorated in pink and brown. Its extra-large window had one-way glass so that its occupant could not be seen from the outside. It was furnished with a bed, three chairs, a table and a wardrobe pushed up against the side wall. The wardrobe was on castors and when moved revealed the door that led directly to the execution chamber; the trap doors through which Ruth would fall were no more than 15 feet from where she slept. On the other side was a bathroom, connected to the next cell which was used for meeting visitors and legal representatives. On 8 July 1955 the *Daily Herald* reported that 'Two goldfish swim in a bowl in the condemned cell… They are fed each day by Ruth Ellis.' No flowers were allowed so Ruth asked that all the bouquets she received be used in the chapel.

Her fate was now in the hands of the Home Secretary, Major Gwilym Lloyd-George. He had been in post since 26 May 1954 when the Conservatives had unexpectedly won the general election. One of their election pledges was the retention of the death penalty.

Immediately after the trial, Ruth spent her time making dolls from the materials brought to her by her mother, doing jigsaws and reading the Bible. She did not drink the beer available to the condemned. To her family she maintained her stance of 'an eye for an eye'. When visitors told her they were sure she would get a reprieve, she seemed annoyed. Bickford, however, acting on her family's instructions, began putting together the case for an appeal.

THE CAMPAIGN TO SAVE RUTH ELLIS

If Ruth phlegmatically accepted her fate, the same could not be said of numerous newspapers and campaigners who were doing everything in their power to make sure that she did not become the fifteenth woman to be executed since the beginning of the twentieth century. Letters flooded in to the press. Sir Beverley Baxter MP wrote to the *Evening Standard* on 6 July 1955 saying: 'If this woman hangs then the shame of it will be upon us all.' The Methodist leader, Dr Donald Soper, writing in the *Daily Herald* on 12 July, stated that 'the killing of a woman would be sordid, shameful and useless' and that 'Christian punishment must be reformatory' (HO 291/271).

Letters and petitions poured into the Home Office (see plates 15 and 16). The senders varied from haulage workers to schoolchildren and came from as far afield as Italy, Belgium, Germany, Denmark, Argentina, France and Norway. Some petitions showed that the senders had gone up and down their street securing signatures; they even persuaded labourers—presumably working on the street—to sign. The letters ranged from the extremely touching to the psychologically disturbed and came from all strata of society. In total, 50,000 signatures were said to have been forwarded.

One letter on 3 July 1955 came from a Mr Fawcett who had been at school with David Blakely and had had the misfortune to sit in front of him. He described David as a sadist:

> The young David Blakely took a positive delight in hurting others. His mercy did not seem to me to exist. I think that if this person's character went on in a progressively worsening way during the last eight years he may well have turned into the sort of person who could so badly hurt someone mentally as to incite that person to lose control of herself and kill him. (HO 291/237)

A playwright called Guy Bolton wrote on 30 June from the Hotel Westminster in Paris:

> If Ruth Ellis is hanged a day will certainly come when the act will be condemned as one of subservience to an outworn legal code. The ladder is a long one and man has mounted slowly from the depths of brutality. When we stood but a dozen rungs lower we acquiesced in the hanging of man for stealing a sheep.
>
> (HO 291/237)

Letters written by men opposing a reprieve were characterized by fears that if Ruth wasn't hanged they were going to have trouble with their wives, while the women who wrote in seemed more concerned about her 'immorality'. An appropriately named E.A. Bitter of Lewisham wrote on 3 July: 'I am married to a woman similar ... to Ruth Ellis, eaten up with jealousy through and through... I greatly fear that my future personal safety would be at stake if you granted a reprieve. PLEASE, DEAR SIR, GRANT NO REPRIEVE' (HO 291/236).

A Mr Brindhlaw of Kentish Town expressed similar feelings in an undated letter: 'I should judge wisely otherwise wifes [sic] will be shooting there [sic] husbands if a woman just says good morning to him ... it would be a riot among wives' (HO 291/236).

Some even sent their own poems. This came in from 'anonymous' on 9 July (HO 291/236):

> Without a prayer from Him or Her
> A young man doomed to meet his Maker
> *CRIME PASSIONELLE* some wildly claim
> And strive to save this female faker.

A famous article appeared in the *Daily Mirror* on 30 June 1955, written by the legendary journalist William Connor under his pseudonym 'Cassandra'. He said of Ruth, in an article which showed a far deeper understanding of the emotions underpinning the murder than had ever been revealed in court:

Pity comes hard after such dreadful deeds…
Yet had I the power I would save her. This was a murder of love
and hate. The one as fierce as the other—the storm of tender-
ness matching the fury of revenge. In human nature where
passion is involved, love and hate walk hand in hand and side by
side. The difference between them is a hair's breadth … the
one can change to the other in a trice. Infinite sweetness and
affection become infinite wickedness and black insensate
cruelty… (HO 291/237)

A *Daily Express* journalist interviewed Raymond Chandler,
who was staying in Eaton Square. The interview was published
on 1 July under the headline: 'Toughest author talks of hanging
Mrs Ellis. Raymond Chandler shocked'. The author said that:

The death sentence on Ruth Ellis has upset me. How can the
British law be so savage? This case of Ruth Ellis was no bestial
or sadistic killing. There was nothing slow about it, like a
poisoning, nothing like the murder of a child. It was a crime of
passion committed, I feel certain under a kind of shock which
may have flared up uncontrollably… The phrase 'cold blooded'
doesn't come into it. This woman was hot blooded. (HO 291/237)

On 28 June 1955 Bickford sent his statement supporting a
plea for a reprieve. In it he stated: 'Each counsel in turn had
an opportunity of meeting the Accused and each was remark-
ably impressed by her outwardly entirely calm demeanour and
her obvious candour. I can vouch for the fact that not only is
she a woman of quite incredible self control and courage: but

she has done her utmost to tell the whole truth so far as she is concerned' (HO 291/237).

CUSSEN, THE GUN AND THE TAXI

Jackie Dyer was among those who did not want Ruth to die. Going to her MP, George Rogers, who had recently been campaigning to clear the name of Timothy Evans, she informed him of what Ruth had told her: that Cussen had made Ruth drunk, taken her to the scene of the crime, placed a gun in her hand and encouraged her to shoot Blakely. When Rogers visited Ruth in prison on 29 June 1955, she reluctantly agreed that he should apply for clemency on her behalf.

The governor of Holloway visited her shortly afterwards and on 30 June wrote the following minute to the Prison Commissioners and the Home Secretary:

> She [Ruth] said he [Rogers] was a great talker and she was too tired to argue with him... she told me she hoped he would fail in his efforts and she would pray that he did. I have never seen Ruth Ellis so distressed, and the officers reported that for the first time she had cried... Principal Officer Griffin reported that she had taken the visit with Ellis and Mr Rogers and that he had 'badgered' her. (PCOM 9/2084)

Griffin also wrote a statement, which was forwarded with the governor's to the Under Secretary of State for Home Affairs on the same date:

> He introduced himself, then said that all her friends and rela-
> tives were distressed at her position. In particular Jacqueline
> Dyer … he kept onto her about living for her child's sake, her
> attitude in wanting to die was all wrong, did she believe in the
> After World, she shouldn't think that by her dying she would be
> with Blakely. She should live to expiate her crime on earth…
> Mr Rogers was so persistent Ellis very grudgingly said, What
> if you do ask for clemency and it fail, I shall still be in the same
> place. Mr Rogers reply was 'I never fail.'

Rogers wrote to the Home Office but—maybe because of these
reports from the prison—his letter was ignored.

However, a letter that Jackie Dyer had written to the Home
Secretary on 25 June 1955 was forwarded to New Scotland
Yard, and she was visited by DCI Davies. He asked her to make
a formal statement, which she did at Hampstead police station
on 1 July 1955: 'We would talk quite a lot about personal matters
and never once did she mention that she had a gun.' Dyer went
on to say that when Ruth gave up her job at the Little Club, 'I
helped to pack her things and I can honestly say that I saw
everything she had. I can swear that there was no gun there.'
She continued: 'During one of my visits to Ruth [in prison] I
gathered from her that Cussen had given her the gun and that
he had driven her to Hampstead on the night of the shooting'
(this and following quotes from MEPO 2/9888).

After interviewing her DCI Davies wrote a long and careful
report about the gun which was forwarded to the Under Secre-

tary of State. His opinion of Jackie Dyer was that 'being a French woman, she finds it difficult to believe that Ellis should pay the supreme penalty for a crime of this nature.'

He confirmed, however, that 'Ellis's story that she had had the gun in her possession for three years was not believed from the outset because of the clean well-oiled condition it was in. As a consequence, inquiries were made to trace its origin but without success.' Later in the same statement he said:

> During the remand period I several times questioned Ruth Ellis as to the authenticity of her story... Throughout she was adamant that this story was true. In view of this we were forced to accept the fact that Cussen did not give the revolver to her.

Then on 6 July a letter arrived at the Home Office from Alexander Engleman, who had been the receptionist at the Little Club. He stated that one night in 1954, 'Cussen was there and asked if he could give me a lift home... outside the club I looked for his car and he pointed to an old taxi which was parked across the road and said this is my car.'

The police traced Cussen, who stated on 9 July 1955:

> I have been asked if I ever owned a taxi cab. I did I bought it early in 1954... I ran it for several months until about June 1954 ... then disposed of it to my brother, William David Cussen ... in about August or September the same year. I have not used it since... I certainly did not drive her to Hampstead that evening, by taxi or otherwise.

The Home Secretary had decided that there should be no
reprieve (see plate 18). His reasons, given on 11 July 1955, are
quoted below in full:

> I have given the most careful and anxious consideration to this
> case.
>
> As I conceive my duty, it is to review all the circumstances of
> a capital case in order to see if there are such mitigating
> circumstances as would justify me in recommending interfer-
> ence with the due course of law. It is no part of the duty of a
> Home Secretary to give any weight to his own approval, or
> detestation of the penalty prescribed by law; and least of all is it
> his duty to alter the law merely on the grounds that he thinks
> that a penalty which is appropriate for a man is inappropriate
> for a woman.
>
> There may be circumstances in a capital case where special
> considerations apply to a woman which would not be applicable
> in the case of a man. A recent example is the case of Mrs Sarah
> Lloyd. I can find no such special circumstances, however, in the
> present case. The crime was a premeditated one and was
> carried out with deliberation. The prisoner has expressed no
> remorse. I can find nothing to justify my taking a less serious
> view of this case than of other similar cases where the crime
> was of a callous and calculated nature.
>
> I have been pressed from many quarters to exercise clem-
> ency in this case on the grounds of the prisoner's sex and of her
> yielding to jealousy which is alleged by some people to be
> stronger in the case of a woman than in the case of a man. But
> our law takes no special account of the so-called *crime*

passionel, and I am not prepared to differentiate between the sexes on the grounds that one sex is more susceptible to jealousy than the other.

Cases may arise from time to time where a husband deserts a wife, or a wife deserts a husband, or where one spouse is deceived by the other spouse in the most provocative circumstances, and clemency may be appropriate in such a case. In the present instance there is no such element: and the woman was as unfaithful to her lover as he was to her.

I have consulted the trial judge and discussed all the details of the case with him. He told me that he was unable to suggest any mitigating circumstances, and although he naturally disowned any responsibility for the ultimate decision, he said that he himself could find no sufficient grounds for suggesting that clemency would be appropriate.

If a reprieve were granted in this case, I think that we should have seriously to consider whether capital punishment should be retained as a penalty.

The fact that many people have signed letters and petitions on behalf of the prisoner is a factor to which I have given due weight. I do not think that it is a conclusive factor.

After much anxious thought I have come to the conclusion that this is a case in which the law should be allowed to take its course. (HO 291/235)

A note from a civil servant initialled 'P.A.' (presumably Philip Allen, Assistant Under Secretary at the Home Office), dated 4 July and contained in the same file, mentioned something else that may have influenced Lloyd-George: 'A serious view has always been taken of the deliberate use of firearms in this country to commit crime, and it is difficult to see what extenuating features there are in this case to warrant a merciful view being taken of this pre-meditated shooting.'

On the same day, the Home Office told the governor at Holloway the news, and she informed Ruth. Now for the first time the reality of Ruth's situation seems to have come home to her: according to both Hancock and Marks and van den Bergh she became hysterical and lay on her bed screaming: 'I don't want to die. I don't want to die.'

John Bickford was the first person to see her, and was in for a shock. As he explained in his statement of 11 June 1972, 'She accused me of deliberately throwing away her case and of having accepted a bribe from Cussen to ensure that she was hanged and he got away free' (MEPO 26/145).

Ruth demanded to see Victor Mishcon, her civil solicitor. Bickford immediately contacted Mishcon, suggesting to him that he ask Ruth about the gun, and the following morning (12 July) Mishcon and Leon Simmons visited her at Holloway. After Ruth had spoken to Simmons about her will, Mishcon asked her if there was anything she wanted to tell them about the gun. Principal Officer Griffin, who supervised the meeting, wrote a report to the governor:

> Mr Mishcon was very persistent in asking Ellis about the gun, stating that it was only fair that the Home Secretary knew the true facts of the gun, he did not suppose it would help Ellis but

the truth could be put on record… after repeated attempts by
Mr Mishcon, Ellis, with very, very great reluctance said alright
I will tell you… (PCOM 9/2084)

The statement Ruth gave was as follows:

I, Ruth Ellis, have been advised by Mr Victor Mishcon to tell
the whole truth in regard to the circumstances leading up to
the killing of David Blakely and it is only with the greatest
reluctance that I have decided to tell how it was that I got the
gun with which I shot Blakely. I did not do so before because
I felt that I was needlessly getting someone into trouble.

I had been drinking Pernod (I think that is how it is spelt) in
Desmond Cussen's flat and Desmond had been drinking it too.
This was about 8.30 p.m. We had been drinking for some time.
I had been telling Desmond about Blakely's treatment of me.
I was in a terribly depressed state. All I remember is that
Desmond gave me a loaded gun. Desmond was jealous of
Blakely as in fact Blakely was of Desmond. I would say that
they hated each other. I was in such a dazed state that I cannot
remember what was said. I rushed out as soon as he gave me
the gun. He stayed in the flat.

I had never seen the gun before. The only gun I had ever
seen there was a small air pistol used as a game with a target.

(HO 291/237)

Having read through the statement, she said: 'There's one more
thing. You had better know the whole truth. I rushed back after
a second or two and said: "Will you drive me to Hampstead?"
He did so and left me at the top of Tanza Road.'

Ruth signed the statement and Mishcon added the time and date: 12.30 pm on 12 July 1955. She then said in passing that during Easter Sunday she, Andre and Cussen had gone to Epping Forest and he had taught her how to fire the gun. This was not added to the statement.

The conclusion to Griffin's report seemed to contradict Ruth's statement: 'She still says she doesn't want to live, if she did, she could have pleaded Insanity at her trial. She said that she went to the flat to seek Desmond. It was her suggestion that she had the gun.'

Whether she wanted to live or not, Ruth was due to be hanged at 9 am the following day, 13 July 1955.

Mishcon immediately telephoned the Home Office to request a meeting. Sir Frank Newsam, the Permanent Under Secretary of State, was at Ascot, so Mishcon saw Philip Allen, the Assistant Under Secretary. Allen phoned Sir Frank at Ascot requesting his return and also phoned DCI Davies, who unfortunately was in bed with flu. In his absence the presence of DC Claiden was requested.

Claiden was interviewed by Allen and presented with the contents of Ruth's statement. He told Allen about the testament of the French teacher, and informed him that the police had been unable to trace the origins of the gun or to find evidence connecting it to Cussen. Asked about the transport used to get Ruth to Tanza Road, he failed to mention that Cussen had once owned a cab. He was then asked whether

Cussen could be charged as an accessory to the crime. He answered yes—if Cussen had known when he gave Ruth the gun that it would be used to shoot Blakely, and more importantly if this could be substantiated by someone other than Ellis, who would be an accomplice in the crime.

The police were instructed to trace Cussen and interrogate him. This they tried and failed to do.

A note on the file initialled 'F.N.' (presumably Sir Frank Newsam) and dated 12 July gives the Home Office view about the last-minute development: 'This uncorroborated statement by the prisoner does not add anything material to the information before the Secretary of State when he decided not to interfere. The discrepancy between the officer's report and Mr Mishcon's statement is interesting and illuminating' (HO 291/237).

In prison on the evening of 12 July 1955 Ruth was writing her last letters (all quoted from Goodman and Pringle). To Jackie Dyer she wrote: 'I am quite happy with the verdict, but not the way the story was told. There is so much people don't know about.' To George Rogers: 'I am quite well—my family have been wonderful. Once again I thank you and your wife. Goodbye.' This was a reference to the fact that Rogers and his wife had taken Andre away to stay with them.

Finally, Ruth wrote to Leon Simmons:

I am now content and satisfied that my affairs will be dealt with satisfactorily. I also ask you to make known the true story regarding Mrs Findlater and her plan to break up David &

I—she should feel content, now her plan ended so tragically…

I did not defend myself. I say a life for a life… I have spoken the truth, and I want you to make the truth known for my family and son's sake.

She also asked that her mother go to David's grave to lay flowers, choosing pink and white carnations—the flower that had figured at other turning points in her life—and asserted that she was well and not worried about anything.

The police meanwhile were keeping a watch on Cussen's flat. Just before midnight Deputy Commander Rawlings told them to withdraw from their position.

The prison governor, Dr Taylor, had written to the prison commissioners shortly after the trial seeking guidance about how the hanging should be carried out. On 26 June 1955 she had been given the advice that:

If the execution is to take place at 9 a.m. … the prison clock chime should be disconnected for the hour of nine… the executioners should be lodged so that they neither have to enter the prison or cross the yards… please inform the Assistant Executioner that he will be eligible for reasonable travelling expenses. Taxi fares will only be payable when public transport is not available. (PCOM 9/2084)

The Home Office was still being bombarded with telegrams and letters. On 8 July a telegram was received from the Women's Social Labour Organization of British Guiana. It ended: 'Consider children alone in the world. Act of mercy will be great boon to International Womanhood' (HO 291/238).

Mrs Gladys Kensington Yule was not in a forgiving mood. In a letter to the *Evening Standard* published on 11 July (two days before the execution) she wrote:

> Don't let us turn Ruth Ellis into a national heroine. I stood petrified and watched her kill David Blakely in cold blood. These hysterical people, getting up petitions for a reprieve, and those rushing to sign them — do they realise that Ruth Ellis shot Blakely to the danger of an innocent passer-by, a complete stranger? As it is I have a partly crippled right hand for life... *crime passionel* indeed! What if other countries would let her off from her just punishment? When has Britain followed the lead of others? Let us remain a law abiding country where citizens can live and walk abroad in peace and safety. (HO 291/237)

Frank Owen, a *Daily Express* journalist, was one of many who felt differently. On 12 July he sent the following telegram to the Home Office (see plate 19):

> Mrs Ellis had a miscarriage three days before she committed murder. If she had given birth to a child and killed it she would have escaped the death penalty under the plea of infanticide. The justification being that her mind had been unhinged by the birth. As it is she shot her lover. Could her mind have been unhinged by reason of the miscarriage? I beg of you to make a last minute decision of mercy. (HO 291/238)

But to no avail. At 6.30 the following morning Ruth made her confession and was administered the last sacrament. She then wrote one last letter to Leon Simmons, which Goodman and Pringle quote by permission of the *Sunday People*:

> Dear Mr Simmons
>
> Just to let you know I am still feeling all right.
>
> The time is 7 o'clock a.m. — everyone (staff) is simply wonderful in Holloway. This is just for you to console my family with the thought that I did not change my way of thinking at the last moment.
>
> Or break my promise to David's mother.
>
> Well, Mr Simmons, I have told you the truth and that's all I can do.
>
> Thanks once again.
>
> Goodbye.
>
> Ruth Ellis.

Ruth spent her last hour kneeling before a crucifix that had been fastened to the wall of her cell at her request.

Hundreds of people had gathered outside the walls of Holloway (see plates 20 and 21); Mrs Violet van der Elst, a campaigner for the abolition of the death penalty, led the chant of 'Evans-Bentley-Ellis'. A few seconds before nine Albert Pierrepoint and his assistant entered Ruth's cell, accompanied by the prison governor, the chaplain and a surgeon. Ruth drank a tot of brandy, her wrists were strapped behind her and she was taken to the adjoining execution chamber. Her ankles were strapped together and Pierrepoint put a white hood over her head. He then adjusted the rope round her neck—and pulled the lever which released the trap doors beneath her feet. Afterwards, in a letter Pierrepoint wrote to Ruth's sister Muriel, he described Ruth as being 'as good as gold' and that 'she died as brave as any man, and she never spoke a single word' (Jakubait).

The medical officer descended the flight of stairs into the pit below the execution chamber and declared Ruth Ellis dead. Her body was then left hanging for an hour.

Pierrepoint dismantled his equipment and was paid 15 guineas. He needed a police escort to leave the prison. Seven months later he was to resign his post as public executioner after an unresolved dispute over pay.

At 9.18 am a warder came out to post the notices of execution on the prison gates. A man held up his child to look. The crowd surged forward, bringing the traffic outside the prison to a halt; mounted police were used to restore order.

After the hour had passed Ruth's body was lowered and made ready for the pathologist, who pronounced that death had been instantaneous, the cause being 'fracture dislocation of the second and third vertebrae' (PCOM 9/2084).

On the same day another article was published by William Connor in the *Daily Mirror*:

> It's a fine day for haymaking. A fine day for fishing. A fine day for lolling in the sunshine. And if you feel that way—and I mourn to say that millions of you do—it's a fine day for a hanging...
>
> In this case I have been reviled as being a sucker for a pretty

face. Well, I am a sucker for all human faces because I hope I
am a sucker for all humanity, good or bad. But I prefer them
not to be lolling because of a judicially broken neck. (HO 291/237)

Ruth's brother Granville was required to identify her body.
Afterwards, he was taken to the governor's office, where the
inquest was held. Outraged by the coroner's repeated use of the
word 'murderess', Granville shouted at him, 'Isn't there something else you can call her?' He was taken from the room and
given a glass of water.

On 27 July Douglas Glover MP wrote to the Home Office
protesting that the incident had been barbaric: 'It is surely bad
enough for any family to know that one of their member is being
hanged, but to demand then that the next-of kin shall come and
see the body seems quite dreadful' (HO 291/238). The Home Office
said it had nothing to do with them; Granville's presence had
been requested by the coroner.

Just 40 minutes after Ruth's death, Louis Tussaud's, the
waxworks in Blackpool, announced that a model of her would be
displayed the next day in its Chamber of Horrors. On 15 July
the *Daily Express* reported: 'In four hours last night, more
than 3000 people queued to see the waxworks—twice as many
as in a normal day.' The *Daily Sketch* noted that 'the dummy is
in a black evening gown, with a black gossamer stole.'

Ruth Ellis was buried in the grounds of Holloway, in a grave
already occupied by four women: Annie Walters, Amelia Sach,
Edith Jessie Thompson and Styllou Pantopiou Christofi.

CHAPTER FIVE

This Beastly Business

Ruth Ellis's hanging created disbelief around the world. She was in many ways the abolitionists' dream: young, pretty and the mother of two small children. (It is striking that there had been far less fuss over the hanging of Mrs Christofi on 13 December 1954. She was aged 51, not particularly good looking, and a Cypriot who spoke poor English.) In America there was agreement that Ruth would not have been executed under any of the laws within the United States. In Australia the Melbourne *Argus* carried an article stating, 'Hanging shames Britain in the eyes of the civilized world'.

The strength of feeling in Sweden was so strong that the ambassador, Sir R. Hankey, wrote to Harold Macmillan on 19 July: 'The campaign in the press has been exceptionally violent—indeed, I can think of no issue since I arrived in March 1954 which has given rise to comparable criticism of our policy or institutions' (FO 371/116897). He quotes several vehement critics, including the newspaper *Aftonbladet*, which stated, 'The reason why we react so very much more strongly when Great Britain is concerned is, of course, that we feel British culture to be nearly the same as ours.'

France was particularly appalled. On 14 July 1955 the *Evening News* reported:

> All the French newspapers today reported the scenes outside Holloway prison and the details of the execution of Ruth Ellis. *Combat* said she had been hanged in spite of public opinion. 'The strictness of British justice in this case appalled the country although it is accustomed to strict laws, many of which originated in the Middle Ages... for the first time perhaps the English have discovered the meaning of a crime of passion such as continental judges often treat with remarkable indulgence...' (HO 291/237)

Only two days later a woman in Corsica also charged with killing her lover was convicted and sentenced to two years' imprisonment. The sentence was suspended and she was released immediately on probation. One French journalist wrote at the time: 'Passion in England, except for cricket and betting, is always regarded as a shameful disease' (date not known; HO 291/237).

Meanwhile the British press condemned various aspects of the case with daily comment. A leader in the *Observer* on the Sunday after Ruth was hanged considered Andre's plight: 'This boy who is fatherless has had something done to him that is so brutal it is difficult to imagine. We should realise that it is we who have done it.'

The *Spectator* was clear about who it blamed for what had

happened. On 15 July 1955 it ran the following leader (the article and correspondence are in LCO 2/5573):

> It is no longer a matter of surprise that Englishmen deplore bull-fighting but delight in hanging. Hanging has become the national sport... The execution of Mrs Ellis has taken place without much disturbance. Mr Lloyd-George, the Home Secretary, has now been responsible for the hanging of two women in the past eight months. This compares with the hanging of 12 women in the previous 54 years. Is this increase of something like 1250 per cent the result of an outbreak of feminine terrorism? Of course not. It is merely the consequence of a weak Home Secretary... Men who go on hanging women, who should not be hanged, can hardly expect to be held in universal esteem...

Lloyd-George was sufficiently incensed to take private advice from Viscount Kilmuir as to whether he should sue. Kilmuir replied, 'as a lawyer, an ex-Home Secretary and an old friend I advise you to let it die in its own stink'.

On 17 July *Reynolds News*, under the headline 'That beastly business', stated:

> Britain will not soon forget Ruth Ellis. But let us remember even more the children of Holloway, who, on the testimony of the local teachers, were in a state of feverish and horrid excitement last Wednesday morning as the minutes ticked by in the death cell near their homes... There are M.P.'s in all parties who won't let him [Lloyd-George] rest on this beastly business.

On 20 July the *Daily Mirror* carried a leader titled 'The Noose Must Go' and announced that in its poll 'Final figures show that of 39,666 readers who voted, 25,845 are AGAINST hanging — a majority of nearly two to one.'

On 21 July the *Daily Herald* quoted Emanuel Shinwell MP as saying, 'The hanging of Ruth Ellis will I am sure, cause a great deal of revulsion of feeling in the country and will bring public opinion round much more against capital punishment.' It also quoted Sylvia Pankhurst: 'It seems to me that when a man is the *victim* the crime is sometimes regarded more seriously than if a woman is killed. This is entirely wrong' (HO 291/237).

On 23 July *The Lancet* published an article on the death penalty:

> The laws against witchcraft were repealed in this country in
> 1736; but they had been recognised, long before that, as an ugly
> piece of humanity, disgracing the statute book. To many of our
> countrymen today, and to the whole peoples of some European
> countries, the death penalty seems as grotesque as did the
> witchcraft laws to 18th century Englishmen... The children ...
> have been dealt a most shattering psychological blow. Any law
> which, in its enforcement, does gross injury to innocent people
> strikes at the whole concept of justice.

The article concluded by saying that 'the perpetual preoccupation with the condemned cell and the gallows is harmful to the mental health of society... Let us hope that those Members of Parliament who have launched a new attempt to get the law changed will succeed in freeing us from this recurrent demoralisation.'

One of these MPs was Sydney Silverman, who had sponsored a clause in the Criminal Justice Bill of 1947 suspending the death penalty for five years, as well as the Death Penalty (Abolition) Bill of 1956. Both were rejected by the Lords. In 1957, however, the Homicide Act first introduced the concept of diminished responsibility. In 1965 the death penalty was suspended for an experimental period of five years and on 16 December 1969, the Murder (Abolition of the Death Penalty) Bill became law. The Ruth Ellis case had focused the public mind on the issue like few others before it; Ruth's life and death had had an impact beyond her wildest dreams.

The case continued to attract attention in other ways. In January 1964 Ruth's prison records were stolen from Holloway when a working party from Pentonville was used to move the documents. The six-inch file was never recovered.

Then in 1971, when rebuilding took place at Holloway, the Home Office was faced with a tricky dilemma. What should they do with the body of Ruth Ellis and the four women who shared her grave? A civil servant, A.P. Wilson, was given the unenviable task of tracking down Ruth's relatives and asking them what they wanted done. He gives a sad description of Andre, 'a nervous, pale faced slightly shabby young man of 26 who looks as though he could do with a good meal' (MEPO 26/145). The Home Office decided that Andre's wishes should be met, and on the night of 31 March 1971 the body was disinterred and moved to St Mary's in Amersham, only a few miles from where David Blakely was buried in Penn. The *Daily Sketch* gave the following account on 2 April: 'There was no marker for the plot. No stone. No card with the flowers. No service. Just Martin Neilson [a name Andre used] muffled in a heavy black overcoat standing silently by the grave.'

A headstone with the name 'Ruth Hornby 1926–1955' later marked the spot.

NEW THEORIES

On 11 June 1972, after what he described as 'all these years of almost ceaseless brooding', John Bickford came forward and gave a statement to the police. He claimed that on Wednesday 13 April 1955 Cussen had told him he had supplied Ruth with the revolver:

> He said that he had cleaned and oiled it. He wiped the bullets and loaded it. He showed her how it worked, his explanation being that she knew he had a collection of three or four guns, she was so beside herself and so persistent and he was so much in love with her that he eventually gave way. (MEPO 26/145)

Cussen went on to state that during Easter Sunday he had taken Ruth to a wood near Gerrards Cross where she had fired at a tree. He then reloaded the gun, throwing the remaining spare bullets and cleaning materials into the Thames. Bickford said that when he confronted Ruth with this, 'She admitted that it was true, but told me that, in no circumstances was he or anybody else to be involved. She said that she had over-persuaded him, because she knew he loved her.'

This version of events fits in with what Ruth said in her statement to Victor Mishcon. And it rings true, unlike theories which have recently tried to portray Cussen as the villain of the piece. The most recent of these is laid out in Muriel Jakubait's book *Ruth Ellis: My Sister's Secret Life*. It is impossible not to feel a great deal of sympathy for the author, but the theory outlined seems utterly implausible. The book suggests that Ruth could not have fired the gun because of the arthritis in her left hand and that it was Cussen, hiding in a bush, who shot David. The trouble with this theory is that five witnesses (Gladys Yule and her husband, Clive Gunnell, David Lusty and George Stephen) claimed to have seen Ruth shoot him. It was also confirmed that he had been killed by bullets from the gun Ruth was holding and which she handed over to PC Thompson. Attempts to portray Cussen as some sort of evil Svengali figure who brainwashed Ruth into killing are equally unconvincing. They presuppose that Cussen was so eager to kill David that he was willing to sacrifice Ruth in the process. That makes no psychological sense at all. Cussen doted on Ruth and was eager to do whatever she wanted.

In 1962 Robert Hancock went out for a drink with Cussen and asked him about the gun. Cussen said: 'If I were writing your book I'd say the man who gave her the gun never thought she'd use it... I think you should say that Ruth told him that she knew someone who would shoot David for her but she had to get a gun for him.'

But according to Ruth's statement Cussen then drove her to Hampstead. Did he really think that she was going to hand the gun over to a hit man? Also, according to Bickford's statement Cussen showed Ruth how to fire it. The most likely explanation is perhaps that he was just doing whatever she asked him to do.

In 1973 the *Sunday People* published Ruth's last statement. It also published the transcript of a tape-recorded conversation between Cussen and Ruth, made by Ruth herself, which had been sold to the newspaper:

> R: I think I've been a fool. I was living with this drip 18 months. Can you imagine it?
>
> C: God, was it as long as that? No wonder you're looking haggard, dear...
>
> R: Shut up or I'll give you a black eye... he's the lowest of the low. Just a little skunk. Rotten to the core... He's just a drip. How he has the nerve to call himself the social life of Buckinghamshire I don't know.
>
> She starts to sing 'I still believe we were meant for each other.'
>
> C: Go to sleep darling. (MEPO 26/145)

Cussen emigrated to Australia in 1964, having sold his share in the family tobacconist business for £10,000. After a number of failed enterprises he moved to Perth and set up a florist's called 'Chez Fleur'. When traced in 1977 by television reporter Peter Williams (who was making a documentary for Thames Television), his business was on the verge of bankruptcy and he was complaining of 'worms in the carnations this autumn'. He denied every point of Ruth's final statement, adding:

> She was a terrible liar you know. Mind you she got her wish.
> She used to complain when I visited her in Holloway that
> they'd cut all the reports of her case out of the newspapers she
> was given to read. She wanted to know the headlines she was
> making. She loved the headlines. She always wanted to be a
> star. She achieved that didn't she? (Marks and van den Bergh)

The human aftermath of the case was predictably tragic. Three months after the hanging, Ruth's sister Betty died suddenly of an asthma attack, aged 18. On 2 August 1958, George Ellis hanged himself with his pyjama cord in a hotel room in Jersey. In 1969, Muriel Jakubait suspects, her mother tried to gas herself; subsequently her mental health deteriorated so sharply that she lived out the rest of her life in a nursing home. John Bickford died of alcoholism in 1977 after a troubled career. In 1982 Andre, after many difficult years struggling to deal with the legacy of his mother's death, committed suicide. He was 37 years old and had led such a solitary life that it was three weeks before he was found. Shortly before his suicide he smashed up his mother's headstone; it was subsequently restored. Christmas Humphreys, aged 81, paid £491 for Andre's funeral.

According to Muriel, for many years Mr Justice Havers sent money to Andre at Christmas.

Georgina, aged three and a half when Ruth was hanged, was adopted by colleagues of George Ellis. She wrote a book called *A Murder of Passion* showing how her life had mirrored her mother's: she had had affairs with George Best and Richard Harris, gave birth to six children and died of cancer in 2001.

In 2003 Muriel Jakubait brought an appeal against Ruth's conviction. The argument put forward by her counsel, Michael Mansfield QC, was that the judge should have allowed the defence of provocation to be put to the jury. On 8 December 2003 the appeal was turned down, and the judges complained that their time could have been spent more productively on cases involving people who were in prison.

Ruth Ellis's hanging was a turning point. The subsequent legal changes rendered British murder law a more emotionally intelligent and compassionate entity than it had been before. It is unlikely today that Ruth would have been found guilty of murder. Not with the history of violence that existed in the relationship, not given that she had been drinking Pernod and taking tranquillizers and had suffered a miscarriage. However, the way that she presented herself in court might well have counted against her. Society still treats women differently from men in court, and women fail to recognize this at their peril.

It is important to remember David Blakely. The many descriptions of him are so deeply unpleasant that it is easy to forget that he was a victim of a brutal killing. No one, however inadequate, deserves to be shot dead at the age of 25. Like many before him, Blakely thought he could take the coward's way out and end a relationship by running away and refusing to communicate. It is impossible to see the photos of his corpse and read the list of his property—which includes 'one metal Toy whistle, six packets of "Whiz Bangs", one pair of sun glasses, one pen knife, one pair of leather mittens' (see plate 8; MEPO 2/9888)—without registering a sense of the human tragedy of his murder.

Ruth Ellis was also a victim: a victim of sexual abuse, of a violent and destructive relationship, and finally of her own sexual obsession. Blakely had cost Ruth her job, her health, her friends, custody of her daughter and her self-respect. He dangled the offer of marriage in front of her, signed a photo and then disappeared in a puff of smoke to spend the weekend with the very people Ruth had asked him not to visit without her. In the end the Home Secretary delivered a judicial 'eye for an eye', which is exactly what Ruth Ellis herself espoused. It's a shame he couldn't have shown her more compassion than she was capable of showing to herself.

It is perhaps fitting to end with a couple of letters from the public (quotes from HO 291/238). On 14 December 1955 Lloyd-George received the following from P.W. Feesey of Raynes Park: 'Of a Father who was a Great Liberal, it is very disappointing to find you a Conservative and Lady Megan transferring to the

Labour party. That explains perhaps, how you arrived at this callous decision; had you been a Liberal, Ruth Ellis may not have hanged.'

On 11 July 1956 Mr Stuart of Ilford wrote to Lloyd-George describing the terrible effect of the hanging on Ruth Ellis's brother. His letter ends with the following quotation from Leo Tolstoy: 'It all lies in the fact that men think there are circumstances when one may deal with human beings without love. But there are no such circumstances… mutual love is the fundamental law of human life.'

Sources & Reading

—

The National Archives has many files on Ruth Ellis. The main Metropolitan Police record is MEPO 2/9888; there also are files about the theft of Ruth's prison records (MEPO 2/10910) and John Bickford's statement in 1972 (MEPO 26/145). The court files are in CRIM 1/2582, and CRIM 8/24 contains press applications for a seat at the trial. Surviving prison records are in PCOM 9/2084, and PCOM 9/1968 concerns the missing prison files. There are Home Office files on the case in HO 291/235–8, while HO 282/58 concerns the exhumation from Holloway Prison (this is also briefly mentioned in T 227/3868). FO 371/116897 documents the Swedish reaction to Ruth's execution, and LCO 2/5573 concerns criticism of Lloyd George in the Spectator.

Books: The best starting point is *The Trial of Ruth Ellis* by Goodman and Pringle. This contains a full transcript of the trial and a clear unsensational account of the events leading to the murder. It also has letters written to the *Evening Standard* 30 June to 12 July 1955, and the debate provoked by the *Lancet* article of 23 July 1955. Of the books written by journalists the most up-to-date is Robert Hancock's *Ruth Ellis, The Last Woman to be Hanged*, originally written in 1963 and updated in 2000. From a personal point of view, some of the most interesting material I found was in Helena Kennedy's classic text *Eve was Framed*, which is required reading for anyone interested in women and British justice, and also Leonora Klein's excellent book *A Very English Hangman*.

G. Ellis (with Rod Taylor), *A Murder of Passion* (Blake, 2003)

J. Goodman and P. Pringle, *The Trial of Ruth Ellis* (David and Charles, 1974)

R. Hancock, *Ruth Ellis: The Last Woman to be Hanged* (Orion, 2000)

C. Hibbert, *The Roots of Evil: A Social History of Crime and Punishment* (Sutton, 2003)

M. Jakubait (with Monica Weller), *Ruth Ellis: My Sister's Secret Life* (Robinson, 2005)

H. Kennedy, *Eve was Framed* (Vintage, 2005)

L. Klein, *A Very English Hangman: The Life and Times of Albert Pierrepoint* (Corvo, 2006)

A. Koestler, *Reflections on Hanging* (Victor Gollancz, 1956)

A. Koestler and C.H. Rolph, *Hanged by the Neck* (Penguin, 1961)

L. Marks and T. van den Bergh, *Ruth Ellis: A Case of Diminished Responsibility* (Penguin, 1990)

A. Pierrepoint, *Executioner Pierrepoint: An Autobiography* (Eric Dobby, 2005)

P. Rawlinson, *A Price Too High* (Weidenfeld and Nicholson, 1989)

E. Tuttle, *The Crusade Against Capital Punishment in Great Britain* (Stevens and Sons, 1961)

Films: Dance with a Stranger (1985), Yield to the Night (1956), Lady Godiva Rides Again (1951)

ACKNOWLEDGEMENTS

The Author would like to thank Catherine Bradley, Gillian Hawkins and Sheila Knight at the National Archives for their enthusiasm and professionalism, also Steve Gove for his meticulous eye for detail.

Pictures can be seen at the National Archives unless another source is given here. **1** Getty Images **2, 17, 20, 21** UPPA/Photoshot **9** Mirrorpix

Index